FOREWORD

Dear Friends of the Far North Line,

My role entails answering many difficult questions: whether I wanted to write the foreword to *FoFNL 25* was not amongst them. I am delighted to have been asked.

The Far North Line has a special place in my heart, as I know it does for its Friends. In 1983, as a sponsored engineering student with British Rail, I used my first free rail pass to travel the length of the line. I was charmed. And whether for work or leisure, I have enjoyed every visit since.

The Far North Line is a fortunate railway. For not only does it pass through some of Scotland's most lovely country, serving communities and places of abiding interest, but it is supported by your most excellent group. As the pages of this special edition record, the Friends of the Far North Line have worked tirelessly to protect, to promote and to develop this railway. And you have done so very effectively.

For Transport Scotland, and for our delivery partners in the ScotRail Alliance, you are critical friends. Your criticisms are fair and well argued; your thanks for the progress we make are much appreciated; and your proposals are always worthy of careful consideration.

Friends of the Far North Line is a benchmark group against which other rail line support groups may be measured.

It is interesting to reflect that your group was formed to address concerns about the future of the Far North Line. Twenty-five years on, there are still challenges to address, but they are of a very different nature. The future of the line is not in doubt. The questions now are about how best to develop the line and its services, both passenger and freight. The Scottish Government understands the contribution this line makes to the economy and communities it serves, and is committed to the line's future success. Track and line-speed improvements; level crossing upgrades; new maintenance staff; and RETB signal developments are all evidence of this. And yes, the investment case for a passing capability between Inverness and Dingwall is under consideration.

So well done the Friends of the Far North Line. What you do matters, and makes a difference. Please keep doing so for the next twenty-five years as well.

With my sincere thanks,

Bill Reeve

Director of Rail
Transport Scotland

FoFNL has had four Presid [...] ian MP, John Thurso MP, Paul Monaghan MP and Jamie S [...] m for helping to keep FoFNL in the forefront of the minds o [...] na.

We currently have three Vice Presidents, all MSPs: Rhoda Grant, John Finnie and Gail Ross. We would like to thank them for their continuous support and for asking lots of questions!

FoFNL has always enjoyed the friendship and support of those we work with in the rail industry and Transport Scotland; we would like to give a special mention to the indefatigable John Yellowlees, currently ScotRail's Honorary Rail Ambassador, a title that couldn't be more appropriate! John is an inexhaustible fount of knowledge about Scotland's railways and those who run them.

25 Years of FoFNL

Welcome to this celebratory survey of the existence and work of the Friends of the Far North Line since our foundation in 1994.

To give a flavour of who we are and what we do we wanted to publish what is, essentially, a special edition of our triannual magazine *Far North Express*. We want to acknowledge the very generous financial support from FoFNL member Andy Adams. Andy, like a sizeable minority of our members, lives nowhere near the Far North Line. His home is in Kent but he belongs to FoFNL as he wishes to see the line prosper; he has paid for the entire cost of printing.

The first section of *FoFNL 25* contains pieces written specially by some of our members, giving their own views about past, present and future.

The bulk of *FoFNL 25* is a kind of timeline, mostly containing items from our newsletter/magazine over the years. This gives a detailed look at the work done by, and the level of knowledge and dedication of, our members. When reading through this it becomes apparent that improving things on the railway can take a very long time indeed!

When compiling the contents I became aware that there is not a great deal of material included from the last few years. There are two reasons for this: many of the earlier items are there to show the kind of things we do all the time; the period since the end of 2016, when Tony Glazebrook's report prompted Fergus Ewing, the Cabinet Secretary for Rural Economy to have the Review Team set up, has been marked by a different kind of activity. From this point on FoFNL has been pushing at an open door. The will to really try and improve the line is genuine and a very large amount of work has been, and at this point is still being, done by Network Rail and ScotRail, led by Bill Reeve, Director of Rail, Transport Scotland. It would not be appropriate to continue to campaign for work which is already in progress. What we do do however, is try and keep the things we hope and expect to be done, in the public eye. Sometimes this feels like a very repetitive exercise!

Ian Budd

Why Far North Line? Why FoFNL?

Why do we have a railway?

Have you ever thought why we have a railway to Caithness, Sutherland and Easter Ross? Did our leaders of the day just want to join the club as it were? In a way, yes, but it was to open up the country and trade with the rest of Scotland and beyond.

Goods traffic (which we now know as "freight") was much more important than passengers. The reasons were more economic than social. North landowners wanted to develop their estates. They promoted private enabling bills in Parliament and financed the railways themselves with wealthy shareholders. Sir Alexander Matheson of Ardross and the Duke of Sutherland were the two outstanding players who established the line north from Inverness. It wasn't until the 1890s that Government funding was made available for the railways with the Kyle and Mallaig extensions.

The railway improved the economic and social health of the Highlands, not least by providing steady employment in both populated and remoter areas. Railwaymen and women have served the area well in the most challenging conditions anywhere in Britain. The Far North and Kyle lines were an invaluable transport asset during both world wars and thrived until the 1950s when competition from road transport started to bite. These roads are provided directly by government of one form or another whereas the railways continue to be expected to provide their own infrastructure.

Since the 1950s the railway has been under threat of closure, with many smaller stations and branches closed in 1960 and the railway north of Inverness earmarked for closure in the Beeching report of 1963. The locally organised MacPuff campaign helped to ensure that the line remained open and the concept of the "social" railway introduced from 1968 has ensured that it has survived other threats since then.

Why do we have FoFNL?

We have to thank Frank Roach, Frank Spaven and the other founding members for this. In 1994 the new road bridges across the firths had captured traffic from rail; freight had ceased; the prospect of privatisation was looming; and what might have been the last attempts to keep alive the idea of a Dornoch rail crossing were being made. It was realised that the line was still under possible threat and needed organised support. Furthermore, it needed users who had ideas to improve services and were organised to promote these.

Frank's idea of a conference was seminal, not to say brilliant, with its inspired objectives. This took place at the Station Hotel in Inverness on 26 October 1995. The outcome was a partnership between the railway with local government and regional development agencies. In 1997 Frank became one of two Highland Rail Partnership development officers for the Highland Lines. Dan McGrory, a career railwayman, became the other responsible for the West Highland Lines. In due course the two posts were combined with Frank Roach in sole charge.

John Melling became Chairman of FoFNL in November 1997 and represented the three line-societies (Far North, Kyle and West Highland) on the Partnership Board. Frank was able to pursue many of the early FoFNL line enhancement ideas and subsequent ones too. He established his office in Lairg Station, able to sell the Highland railcard and provide information to passengers there. Re-openings such as Beauly and Conon Bridge stations and the Invernet commuting trains have been well documented in our magazines. Pump priming for consultancy studies and for new services have all helped to advance development of the line and its connections from south (Perth) and east (Aberdeen).

The largest study was *Highland Rail Room for Growth Study* completed in March 2006 which was commissioned by Highlands and Islands Enterprise from Scott Wilson and covered all the routes to and from Inverness and also the West Highland lines. This was needed to inform the Scottish Government's Strategic Transport Projects Review published in December 2008 because Network Rail's Route Utilisation Strategies for Scotland were not going to cover the Highlands. *Room for Growth* has proved to be invaluable and many of the recommendations are still being worked on for STPR2 in 2019.

John Melling was succeeded by Richard Ardern as Friends' representative on the Highland Rail Partnership (HRP) Board in February 2004. HRP became a Company Limited by Guarantee in February 2005 and was finally wound up in August 2009. Frank had transferred to HITRANS in 2008 to be their Partnership Manager responsible for rail services. Over twenty five years of valuable service to rail developments in the Highlands, which all started with his forming of FoFNL, is a record of which he can be proud!

FoFNL continues meantime under the Convenership of Ian Budd who has run the website for most of FoFNL's 25 years and is now producing the *Far North Express* to such high standards that it won the Best Newsletter Award from the UK campaigning body Railfuture in 2017.

Why do we have FoFNL? There are many reasons, but we could not do without it now.

Richard Ardern

We begin our survey of the last 25 years of FoFNL with a poem - a heavily annotated poem, but it's worth reading through the notes at the end as they give a good insight from someone who has been in from the start...

Lines on Celebrating Twenty Five Years of FoFNL by 'Salzcraggie'

'Twas in the year nineteen ninety-three
While a baby was balanced upon a knee
In a caravan for three in Rogart Station yard[1]
A call came through from Ian Jamieson[2]
In response to a *P&J* letter calling for a new approach
With Dornoch road bridge built[3]
And as privatisation encroached
What future for the Far North Line amid the change?
Fourth summer train cut[4], Thurso depot[5] no more
Georgemas splits ending[6] -
The line needed befriending.

With Dornoch men Millar[7] Spaven[8] and Moore[9]
The Friends of the Far North[10] were formed
Their battle cry Tain Commuter[11] Freight[12] and Steam![13]
With Bob Maclennan in the van[14]
And Stop the Railway Madness[15] abroad
We pressed, we released, we interviewed,
We conferenced in 95[16]
To demonstrate we had truly arrived,
With samizdats produced on Dingwall Academy's computers[17]
Pressed into the hands of hard-pressed commuters.
The Friends linked with HRP[18]
The Far North was not forgotten you see
With Tain[19], Sunday trains[20], 158s[21], Beauly[22]
The privatised industry found us an ally.[23]
Invernet[24], Conon[25], and toilet retention[26]
And soon to be Lentran[27] gain a mention
Thanks to the attention of the FoFNL,
And the Great Helmsdalemen Lunan, Brandon, Budd and J Mell.[28]

In '99 the 125th was sung with a 158 run.[29]
150 beckons in 2024[30]; the Friends will be there
At the going down of the sun -
A Highland survivor[31] amid the fallen:
BR, NX, FSR, Railtrack and FEng.[32]
Who will remember them?

[1] The Roaches moved into Rogart Station House in Jan 1993, then moved out during renovations.

[2] Rail enthusiast running B&B in Inverness, first Treasurer of FoFNL

[3] Opened in October 91, hopes of a combined road/rail bridge were thwarted by the Scottish Office

[4] Winter was an Invergordon terminator, but in high summer 4 car ran to Caithness, returning very late

[5] Chris Green had considered shutting Wick and bussing folk to Georgemas; the current arrangement keeps Wick on the network

[6] From memory a split in the 10xx from Inverness last took place in 1998

[7] Harry Millar Tain Councillor was the first Chair of FoFNL. The three had originally met with others to try to get the combined bridge back on the table

[8] Frank Spaven was the civil servant who effectively advised Ministers in 1963 not to propose closure, later head of Planning and Research at HIDB

[9] John Moore was a bluff Yorkshireman who regretted not to have been born when his father worked at Inverness depot; he later joined DORLAG

[10] Much based on FoSCL- the author experienced a Damascene moment at Garsdale Signalbox in 1976, had been a long-standing member and had met its luminary Ruth Annison at Hawes

[11] Tain Commuter nearly happened in 1997, but BRB would not allow it (despite Highland Council funding) to jeopardise the economics around the letting of Franchise One. Instead the 98 Dingwall Commuter became the first new service in the privatised era in Scotland

[12] Transrail ran a weekly train in September 95 carrying coal, flagstone, steel for Norfrost, freezers, pipe etc which led to the Safeway Flyer

[13] FoFNL helped to set up Highland Railway Heritage which ran steam on the line in 1999

[14] A huge debt is owed to Bob, now Lord Maclennan, Caithness and Sutherland MP whose endorsement of the group was vital

[15] STORM was an anti-privatisation movement with Bill Williams and Maxwell Macleod organising gatherings around the North

[16] Station Hotel Inverness was the venue with speeches from Bob Maclennan, Charles Kennedy, Brian Wilson, John Ellis, Paul Salveson, Julian Worth

[17] With the assistance of Roger Piercy, later newsletter editor

[18] FoFNL represented in multi- agency Highland Rail Network Development Partnership which morphed into Highland Rail Partnership

[19] Dingwall Commuter extended back to Tain in 2000

[20] Winter all year-round Sunday service from 2001

[21] 156s replaced in 2000

[22] Beauly opened in 2002 after a bit of wrangling over short-platform operating procedure - 3rd busiest station in the line after DIN and MOO. 723000 passengers since 2004

[23] A debt here is owed to the formidable and omniscient John Yellowlees and his mentor John Boyle without whom etc etc...

[24] Started 2005, 2006 4th southbound at 08xx to connect with the Stromness ferry (well done Richard Ardern) Invernetxtra 2008 with 4th train now in both directions

[25] Conon Bridge opened 2013 with funding from Kessock Bridge works mitigation

[26] 158s no longer dropped waste on the tracks in 2009 following Mike Lunan's debut on Radio 5 Live

[27] See [24] above - an obsession that may become reality post Far North Line Review Team

[28] Chairs who held the rail in position while others were sleepers - Mike Lunan twice, John Melling, John Brandon and the newsworthy Ian Budd

[29] The train complete with on train dining ran to time despite folk joining at every station (not by chance, that)

[30] The railway to Wick fully opened on 28 July 1874

[31] By David Spaven - available at all good bookshops

[32] British Railways (later British Rail) 1948-97, National Express 1997-2004, First ScotRail 2005-15, Railtrack 1994-2002, First Engineering 1995-2008 (now Babcock)

All organisations like FoFNL require not only some visionaries who recognise the need for something to be done, but also a good supply of people with expertise and useful knowledge who are willing to volunteer to work for the desired outcomes.

FoFNL has had a good supply of both over these 25 years and the first part of FoFNL 25 contains a selection of pieces either by, or about, some of them.

FoFNL's first chairman was **Harry Miller**. Here is an extract from the obituary published in the June 1999 *FoFNL Newsletter*.

Henry (Harry) Miller 1927 - 1999

Harry was born in Caithness, where after acquiring his own farm holding at Forss he went on to become a respected figure in the farming community. In 1962 he bought a farm near Tain and moved to Easter Ross. It was then that he developed his other great interest, politics and public service. He was elected to Tain Town Council in 1969 and was to go on to serve Ross and Cromarty and Highland Regional Councils, holding committee chairmanships. He was a Justice of the Peace and a member of the Cromarty Firth Port Authority. It was almost at the end of his active life that Harry became the first chairman of The Friends of the Far North Line, a position from which he retired in 1997.

FoFNL's first Treasurer and Membership Secretary was **Ian Jamieson**. It was his zealous recruitment over breakfast one winter's morning of a lone resident at his guest house which produced FoFNL's current Convener and Magazine Editor!

The editor has asked me, as a founding member, to record some of my early impressions of FoFNL for this special edition. As I no longer have my written notes from those days most of what follows will be from memory, although I have also made reference to the early editions of the newsletter.

Early in 1994 Frank Roach posted a short letter in the Inverness Courier suggesting that if the Far North Line were to survive, a support group needed to be formed, in much the same way as the Friends of the Settle and Carlisle Line had successfully been, and would anyone who was interested please telephone him.

Recognising the validity of his argument I rang Frank to register my interest and a few weeks later, a meeting was convened at Rogart Station to discuss the proposal. Around seven or eight of us crammed into Frank's sitting room, and there ensued a lively debate as to the best way forward.

Arising from this initial meeting, Frank came to see me about a week later and asked if I would be prepared to act as Treasurer/Membership Secretary while he would act as Secretary. I was quite happy to fulfil this dual role and we were thus able to start a membership base formed from interested groups and individuals. It was also realised that a simple brochure would be required to send to new members and it was left to me to design this, with a schematic map and a brief description of the history of the line.

The next requirement was to invite a high-profile person to be president of the society so Frank approached The Rt Hon Robert Maclennan MP who readily agreed to fulfil that role.

Next, a committee had to be formed. Several early FoFNL members were obvious choices and the original committee consisted of the following. Harry Miller (Tain), Frank Spaven (Inverness), John Moore (Fortrose), John Melling (Inverness), Frank Roach, and myself - with apologies if I have forgotten anyone. At that time, my wife and I owned a large guest house in the centre of Inverness, and, having a large lounge available, it was decided that committee meetings would be held there, for the time being at least.

This had all happened by the Autumn of 1994, so it can be seen that a fair bit

Frank Spaven

of ground had been covered in just a few months and Frank managed to publish the first newsletter in September 1994, with others following in December 1994 and March 1995.

The first AGM was held on 12th November 1994 when eleven members were present, with eight apologies received. Various matters were discussed and one of the key issues that emerged was the possibility of staging a conference as soon as possible to highlight the potential of the Far North Line and to acquaint individuals and groups with FoFNL and its stated aims. In particular it was decided to attract the interest of the various tourism bodies such as Highlands and Islands Enterprise (HIE), Ross and Cromarty Enterprise (RACE), and Caithness and Sutherland Enterprise (CASE), together with District Councils, Community Councils, Chambers of Commerce, Business, ScotRail, Railtrack, Rail Unions, Scottish Natural Heritage, and other environmental and community groups.

After some intense organisation, principally by Frank, the Station Hotel in Inverness was booked for Thursday, 26th October 1995 and invitations sent out in June to as many organisations as possible, including all those mentioned above. The cost, including lunch, was £45 per head, with concessions at £25. Advertised speakers were Robert Maclennan MP, Donald Macpherson (Area Manager, ScotRail), John Holwell (Transrail), and Dr Paul Salveson (Transnet).

The conference was generally felt to be most worthwhile and this was summed up by Donald Macpherson, when he wrote to FoFNL as follows, "Just a short note to thank you for the excellent conference in Inverness last Thursday. The quality and variety of the speakers was excellent and it was extremely encouraging to see all the major bodies committed to working together to improve railway services in the Highlands."

In retrospect, the conference must be seen as pivotal, both for FoFNL, and for the Far North Line itself. Much good work has been achieved since, with several of our more ambitious aims being realised. Other pressures led to me rescinding the office of Treasurer/Membership Secretary, while Frank's appointment within the railway industry necessarily led to his resigning his position. I am sure that I speak for both of us when I say how grateful we are to all those who have so effectively carried forward the work initiated by us in 1994.

'Would FoFNL have been formed if someone had not had the foresight to encourage its establishment twenty-five years ago? Well, yes. Probably someone else would have realised the necessity of forming such a support group, but FoFNL exists today thanks to the flair and organisational ability of Frank Roach to whom we must accord our deep appreciation.

Ian Jamieson

Roger Piercy was FoFNL's second Newsletter Editor and produced every edition from February 1998 to May 2011. Our web archive dates from Roger's first newsletter and provides a fascinating insight into FoFNL's work. The Timeline in this publication is mostly taken from material that appeared therein.

FoFNL Memories

Nineteen ninety four was a memorable year for me as I met Frank Roach for the first time in the staff room of Dingwall Academy where he had arrived to teach French. Making him welcome I soon discovered that we had a common interest in railways, mind you, his went further than mine in that he had bought Rogart Station house and was prepared to travel each day, often by bike! The subject soon got round to his setting up of FoFNL and the next thing I knew, I became member 14.

Communication with members was via a newsletter but as Frank hadn't yet made it into the digital world of Desk Top Publishing (DTP) and having acquired the first of the Apple mac computer his creations were interesting in that he used the cut and paste method – literally, with newspaper cuttings having to be pasted on sideways to get them to fit. Being heavily involved in Computing in the Academy I often suggested that the presentation could be improved and one of my 6th year pupils was tasked to

9

experiment with DTP, but unfortunately just as the first digitised copy was about to be produced the files were lost.

By now I had become conversant with DTP, producing my local Community Newsletter, and I suggested to Frank that I would be willing to take on the role of compiler, naively thinking that we could exchange material in the staff room, but it wasn't to be.

The Annual General Meeting of 1998 was the next significant stage in my involvement with FoFNL. At that AGM John Melling was elected to the office of Chairman. Having introduced my offer of becoming involved with the newsletter to the meeting, Frank announced that he would be leaving Dingwall Academy for a newly created job as Highland Rail Development Officer with Highland Rail Partnership. My offer was taken up with me left wondering how the exchange of material etc was to take place. Just as I was about to leave, John Melling announced that there was to be a short Committee Meeting and would I wait to hear the result, and, yes, you've guessed it, the Committee decided that the Editor of the newsletter had to be a Committee Member.

And so commenced 13 years of stimulating, sometimes frustrating experiences of railway life in the Highlands.

The original method of printing was photocopying with the inherent disadvantage of poor reproduction of photographs but by issue 14, September 1999 we had moved on to inkjet printing of the cover. In January 2000, issue 15 we used an outside printer to produce a glossy cover, still in black and white but the big change came with issue 18 when the cover was inkjet colour printed. The whole operation was done in-house with the inner pages printed on a fast laser printer with the collating, stapling, envelope stuffing and stamping all being done on the dining-room table – happy days!

I am constantly reminded of the Line in that I can hear the warning 'whistle' for the Foulis crossing, across the Firth, as I labour in the garden and if continuous welded track ever gets installed then I will miss the 'clicks' over the rail joints.

Roger Piercy

Keith Tyler, former Secretary of FoFNL, literally put Kinbrace on the map, through his letters to the national and the railway press. Keith became Secretary of FoFNL in January 1998, taking over from Founder Secretary, Frank Roach, who had become the Rail Development Officer. He died at his home, Kinbrace Station House, late in 2011.

In this picture of the FoFNL Committee arriving for a meeting Keith can be seen peeping out of his front door!

Photo: Richard Ardern

FoFNL Newsletter, June 1998

FACING POINTS

A contribution from our Secretary.

As an 'incomer' - though a regular visitor for longer, I have lived at Kinbrace for barely three years - and one for whom the railway is a lifeline against the encroachments of bad weather and a senior age bracket, I was quickly impressed by FoFNL's record over a relatively short period in building sound relationships and thereby securing improvements in the service.

And it is only fair, before going any further, to add a few words of appreciation for the excellence of Far

North Line operation, not only in punctual and reliable running and trolley service, plus the maintenance and cleaning input and the work by Railtrack that makes all this possible, but also, and above all, the unfailing courtesy, resilience and helpfulness of on-board staff. Within the context of ScotRail's reputation for enriching today's travel experience, our line is as good as any. FoFNL would of course like to see such improvements as reduced travel time by upgrading level crossings and even modest realignments to ease the incidence and/or severity of some speed restrictions. We would be glad to get a few more stations reopened; so perhaps this is essential if any overall gain is to be achieved over the status quo. We must be practical. Anyone with a few million pounds they are unsure how to invest might find Railtrack not wholly unappreciative - even, who knows, willing to consider rescheduling the priority of such matters!

If at some time we are seeking to make a point that is, say, not too welcome or appears over-ambitious, it is not surprising to be asked "Well what sort of a group are you? Who do you represent? Why should we listen to you?" It strengthens our credibility to be able to prove that we are a broadly based Society and by no means a pressure group with an obsessive and limited outlook. We should be setting out now to increase our membership substantially. And in this of course every member can help. If you are not already doing it - I know some of you are - make your membership well known, and by your good will and enthusiasm encourage others to join us. It could just be - the signs are there - that the tide is beginning to turn in favour of railway development, so let's see if we can help it to come in with a will.

Keith Tyler

Dr. Stewart Campbell has a long history of membership of the FoFNL committee having served two spells.

This is the announcement in the January 2001 issue of our newsletter that Stewart was rejoining the committee:.

DR. STEWART CAMPBELL

Some of you may remember that Dr. Stewart Campbell has already served one term as a committee member and to bring you up to date I have included a 'pen picture' of his background and interest in railways.

Railways are in his blood. One of his earliest sound memories is of the nightly unfitted scrap metal train to Glengarnock Steel Works which always ran out of steam on the incline outside his house in the late forties. The Station was the hub of the community. He could hear the signal dropping - time to finish breakfast and run.

He came by train to Alness for his interview as a G.P. 25 years ago from which he has only just retired. That day he could not believe his luck in coming to such a beautiful place with its reopened railway station.

He soon found himself attending the Alness Community Association and with help managed to get the local bus to call at the Railway Station at train times. They also got 50 signatures of people who would support a Commuter Train! That was 25 years ago. The station became vandalised and was burned down and Beeching marched across the land with his brand of corporate vandalism. Those were the Dark Days.

The sun is however shining once again. He is now a volunteer Sustrans Ranger and the railway of his childhood memories is now part of National Cycle Network Route 7 from Inverness to Dover. It has not been difficult for him to enthusiastically combine his love of railways with his love of cycling and walking.

Stewart has now retired, earlier than intended and hopes to make a contribution to the health of the community by promoting exercise and sustainable transport particularly by encouraging 'joined up travel'. His ambitions include seeing hordes of people walking and cycling to catch the Tain Commuter Train, many more lorry loads transferred from the A9 to the railway and crowds of tourists coming north by train to walk and cycle.

11

COMMITTEE WORK

Photo: Richard Ardern

[Left] Frank Roach arrives in a healthy fashion to talk to the FoFNL Committee in Inverness.

[Right] FoFNL sponsored the Jellicoe commemorative plaque at Thurso station. The unveiling took place on 5 October 2017, seen here are John Jellicoe, Jamie Stone MP (FoFNL President) , Mike Lunan (Convener) and Captain Chris Smith.

Photo: Richard Ardern

Angus Stewart, our second Membership Secretary, took over from Frank Spaven in 2001. This was how he was introduced to the members in our newsletter:

ANGUS STEWART

Angus Stewart was born, and has lived in, St Andrews for most of his life. His lifelong passion for railways was nurtured at a very early age by frequent visits with his mother to St Andrews station, resulting in many trips on the footplate as the locomotive ran round its train for the return trip to Leuchars. As his mother came from the Isle of Iona there were many family trips to the island by train via Glasgow to Oban then ferry to Mull, bus to Fionnphort and finally motorboat! This fostered an interest in the Highlands of Scotland as a whole and its railways. Days of scouting/scout leadership led to trips on many, now closed lines and expeditions to the Highlands. After marriage and the ownership of a car many less accessible areas were explored countrywide.

On a trip to reconnoitre the caravan site at Brora a night was spent at Rogart in Frank Roach's converted coach which led to an introduction to the Friends of the Far North Line. As his particular interest is current railfreight, visits to Inverness/Fort William and all points on the lines North feature frequently on his itinerary.

Angus is also a very keen railway modeller with a special interest in Austrian/German models. He is current secretary of Glenrothes Model Railway Club which participates in many railway exhibitions and is a past president and secretary of St Andrews Railway and Transport Society.

One of FoFNL's longest-standing members - No. 28, **Daniel Brittain-Catlin** is Deputy Editor, BBC Parliament. He joined FoFNL at Frank Roach's inaugural meeting in the Station Hotel, Inverness in 1994 and is a familiar figure on the line. He can be found at Dunrobin Castle Station on Open Days in the summer.

Daniel is seen here with Michael Portillo, who visited the station whilst making an episode of *Great British Railway Journeys* in 2012.

FoFNL 25th Anniversary

It was only a very short advertisement in the Sunday Times property section which I read over breakfast at home in Clackmannanshire in August 1988, but the message was clear: Scotscalder station building was for sale.

After a week of directing STV's Edinburgh Festival coverage I found myself on the Edinburgh-Inverness sleeper (hope it won't be long until it's back and extended to Thurso). After breakfast it was on to a distinctly old-school train hauled by a class 37 to Scotscalder scheduled at an impressively slow speed.

And so began my association with the Far North Line, endlessly enjoyable and sometimes frustrating. The first of those frustrations came in 1989 mid-way through the restoration of the building. The Ness bridge collapsed and the extra joy of a bus trip to Muir of Ord became an integral part of the journey. It was not disappointing when that ended.

My first contact in the area was Lewis Sinclair, a member of the local track gang, who stays up the road. He and his late wife Christine have a long family history on the railway, and I noticed early on that the two redundant Scotscalder signal cabins had gravitated to his garden. My proudest moment was when he gave me the old loo seat from the gents. Lewis has an inexhaustible number of fascinating memories about the railway and the part it played in the area. He offered me the utmost help during the building restoration, very pleased to see the station come to life again.

The arrival of Frank Roach in 1993 and the founding of the FoFNL the following year were exactly what the line needed. Both have played a vital part in the life of the line and without them its survival could easily have come under extremely close scrutiny.

Of course once I'd discovered Scotscalder, there was a huge area to be explored. It wasn't long until an agreement was reached with the Sutherland Estates to take on the restoration of Dunrobin station and its conversion to a museum. (www.scotlandrailholiday.com/dunrobin) . With huge regret I sold Scotscalder in 2004 but am glad to say Dunrobin is still going strong....a bit too strong, as there's no space left for exhibits. On 11 May 2019 the arrival of the Steam Dreams London-Dunrobin charter brought an exceedingly busy day. 2020 will see the 150th anniversary of the opening of the Duke of Sutherland's Railway, so we shall have to think of an appropriate way to celebrate. In the meantime if you have not visited the museum, look out for the next open days - hope to see you there.

Daniel Brittain-Catlin

David Spaven

We are fortunate to have had much help over the years, particularly on freight matters, from David Spaven, who joined the FoFNL Committee in 2017. David is the Scotland Representative of the Rail Freight Group. He is also the author of many fine railway books including three about the Waverley Route (Borders Railway) and *The Railway Atlas of Scotland: Two Hundred Years of History in Maps* - a wonderful volume!

Here, as an introduction to the piece he has written for *FoFNL 25*, is our review of his definitive history of the Far North Line, *Highland Survivor*. His book was later awarded the title of Railway & Canal Historical Society's *Railway Book of the Year 2017*.

It would be hard to think of anyone better-qualified to write this book. David Spaven has worked on the line, written several important books about railways, is a FoFNL Committee member and the son of FoFNL's founding Vice President, Frank Spaven, who was instrumental in saving all the main lines north of Perth from closure in the 1960s.

The book is in three very logical sections: Before Beeching, The Beeching Era and After Beeching.

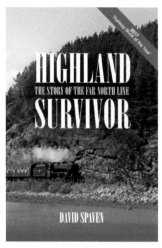

The first part explains exactly what led to the Beeching Report and how it affected the FNL and would be a very worthwhile read even for someone for whom the FNL holds no special interest.

Part two vividly portrays the struggle to save the line and the sometimes conflicting elements of that struggle. This is where Spaven's personal knowledge is invaluable. The final section of the book charts the progress of the FNL since its reprieve and brings into sharp focus the changes which have occurred and which have led to the difficult situation which the Scottish Government and the ScotRail/Network Rail Alliance are now having to address.

Spaven has laid out what he thinks needs to happen urgently, and the consequences of doing nothing. This has led to some fairly robust assurances from official quarters and, most importantly, has linked in with our own campaigning, to the point where major action to improve things now looks likely.

Highland Survivor is required reading for all concerned in any way with the FNL - as users, campaigners, politicians or observers and is a thoroughly enjoyable read.

Ian Budd

Freight Fortunes

When my father Frank responded to Frank Roach's visionary call – in early 1994 – to establish a support group for the Far North Line, the importance of freight to the railway was never far from his mind. Based on long experience professionally as a civil servant advising on railway policy, and personally as a rail development advocate, he understood only too well that railways – with their expensive, specialised infrastructure – are inherently volume-hungry.

That understanding had been reinforced by the findings of a post-retirement MSc thesis at Aberdeen University on 'The role of rail transport in the development of highland regions in Scotland, Norway, Sweden and New Zealand'. To justify their subsidy by government, secondary routes in rural areas had to be multi-purpose – and not just passenger operations.

This was highly pertinent to the circumstances of the Far North Line in the mid-1990s. The completion of the road-only Dornoch Firth Bridge in 1991 had exposed the railway north of Tain to even stronger competition. And the longstanding barley traffic from eastern England to the Muir of Ord silo (for the nearby maltings) which had eventually resumed after the Ness Bridge hiatus, by 1994 had fallen foul of the process of smoothing the path towards rail privatisation, when even individual trainload flows were discarded if they did not meet a target eight per cent notional return on capital.

My own connection to the Far North Line is also very much freight-related. I began 40-plus years ago working in and around the rail industry in the summers of 1973 and 1974 at Invergordon and Tain at a time when the area was a hotbed of rail freight activity, following the 1971 opening of the Invergordon aluminium smelter.

Far North Line freight has seen many ups and downs since these halcyon days, and it is worth reflecting in particular on the key trends since the early 1990s to try to understand better how we can help to ensure that freight is firmly at the heart of future rail operations between Inverness and Caithness. And since joining the FoFNL Committee, I have been heartened by colleagues' solid support for freight expansion – despite those frustrating occasions when a freight train failure screws up the passenger service!

Decline and fall, then revival and retrenchment

When the Ness Bridge fell into the river in 1989, freight had already become a shadow of its former self 15 years earlier. By 1988 – the year that Lentran loop was shortsightedly closed – there was just a single daily freight north of Inverness (to Invergordon / Lairg). The loss of freight traffic resulting from the closure of the smelter in 1982 had been compounded in 1984 by the cessation of all domestic coal traffic to 10 depots along the length of the route. The traditional wagonload train to Caithness could not survive the loss of baseload coal business.

However, the reassuring replacement of the Ness Bridge in 1990 soon brought an early intimation of a future sustained freight flow, with a temporary rail contract for movement of steel pipes for the offshore oil industry from Hartlepool to Georgemas in 1991. The first general freight train to run through to Caithness for 11 years was operated in 1995, and this initial flow developed into a regular weekly 'Enterprise' wagonload service in 1996, provided by EWS, the new, private rail haulier. That same year, what had been in late 1995 a trial trainload movement of large steel pipes from Hartlepool to Georgemas – for fabrication at the nearby Rockwater yard – became a regular (initially twice-weekly) service. The weekly Enterprise train conveyed a wide variety of traffics, including fridges and freezers, steel plate, agricultural lime, containerised aviation fuel and timber to and from a variety of railheads on the Far North Line.

Photo: Sandy Colley

In 1999 the supermarket company, Safeway, pioneered the rail movement of supermarket supplies with its daily Mossend-Inverness train, and the following year the concept was extended northwards to Caithness. But bad news followed good news in 2000. EWS shareholder pressure for commercial returns led to a first rationalisation of the Enterprise network that year, including withdrawal of wagonload services from all the timber terminals established over the previous eight years on the Far North Line. The loss of timber abstracted volume from the Caithness train service just when its frequency had been increased from weekly to daily to meet Safeway requirements.

Photo: Duncan Stewart

However, in 2002 regular oil traffic returned to Lairg, as part of a £10m FFG award to BP Oil UK Ltd for upgrading the facilities at the Grangemouth refinery and five distribution railheads across Scotland. And, learning from the pioneering 'lineside loading' of timber by BR on the West Highland Line in the 1980s, a £100,000 project was developed by the Highland Rail Partnership and others to construct a 250-metre-long loading pad adjacent to the Far North Line, just south of Kinbrace. The first train ran in 2002, then developed into a pattern of running five nights a week every third week during the summer, with timber distributed by road from the Inverness railhead to various local users. While lineside loading minimised capital expenditure, it involved very high operating costs, partly through catering for the complexity of night-time working (and the associated intense peak of loading activity, and double-handling of the timber), and also through the cost of detaining a £2m locomotive on site for several hours while the train was loaded.

In 2005 external market changes (to which rail is always vulnerable) led to the abrupt end of the daily train to Caithness, with rail becoming a casualty of the takeover of Safeway by Morrison and the subsequent enforced sale of its Caithness stores to the Co-op, which had different supply chain arrangements. Without the (admittedly small) Safeway baseload, the rail economics could not be made

to work. In any event, the nationwide Enterprise wagonload network was steadily shrinking in the face of unprofitable operation. Once more, the Far North Line lost its mixed freight service, although the full trainloads of pipes, with their much superior economics, continued to operate from Hartlepool to Georgemas.

2005 also saw the end of the Kinbrace-Inverness trainload timber flows. The complexity, cost and risk associated with providing a reliable rail service, for relatively modest volumes of around 15,000 tonnes a year, proved to be too high for the Flow Country's timber markets to bear.

Thereafter, freight on the Far North Line has essentially been restricted to pipes to Georgemas, nuclear movements from Georgemas and the reinstated Grangemouth-Lairg oil flow until its sad demise in 2018.

Photo: Sandy Colley

Efforts to re-start timber flows – there have been none on rail in Scotland since 2009 – have suffered from, on the one hand, the cost of creating convenient, well-equipped terminals in forest areas, and, on the other hand, the operational and commercial inflexibility of lineside loading. Whereas in the past the rail industry has been criticised for its inability or unwillingness to meet market needs, more recently the focus has switched to the onus on forestry companies to work collaboratively in order to create viable trainload flows. As Frank Roach reminded delegates at the 2016 Timber Transport Conference in Perth, the public sector in the shape of HITRANS had devoted considerable time and resources to developing the concept of timber by rail from the Flow Country. He was convinced that rail could deliver a solution: did forestry interests now want to 'get on track' or would they 'remain in a siding'?

Future prospects

Over and above timber, a regular service to and from Caithness would be attractive for a wide range of intermodal and bulk commodities, including supermarket supplies, oil, compressed natural gas and cement.

The grain distillery at Invergordon was deliberately sited astride the railway in 1961. While it is now 27 years since regular movement of bulk spirit from the north of Scotland to Central Scotland maturation plants was undertaken by rail, Invergordon's current capacity is 38 million litres of pure alcohol per annum, which equates to some 25 road tankers a week, a potentially important contribution to a daily trunk train service from the Inner Moray Firth and Speyside areas to Central Belt maturation plants.

FoFNL's policy statement on freight (see page 69) sets out the key infrastructure and service measures which are needed if the line if to realise fully its undoubted freight potential. My father would doubtless have endorsed these, as part of his wider understanding of opportunities for the region's railways. Within the conclusions of his 1989 thesis, he concluded more broadly that: 'The highlands [sic] are difficult country for railways but they have proved their worth as secondary main lines.' In a later (1991) reflection – in the context of the prospects for re-opening a railway to the Borders – he commented on the latter region having 'the resources potential for "tourists and timber", which my researches in Norway, Sweden and New Zealand have shown to be a winning traffic combination for Highland-type lines.' Let us hope that his vision becomes reality on the Far North Line.

David Spaven

Richard Ardern, a retired geographer and librarian, is one of Scotland's leading rail advocates. Besides his long-standing membership of the FoFNL committee he is involved in several other organisations, and was a director of the erstwhile Highland Rail Partnership. Richard contributes several items in each edition of Far North Express and his wide knowledge and experience is invaluable.

Richard was the last 'Chairman' before the title was changed to 'Convener' in 2005. He describes himself as "merely an amateur"!

POLICIES AND REPRESENTATION(S)

Being Chairman or Convener of FoFNL is an honour and a responsibility. There is the opportunity to do so much to try and encourage government and the rail businesses to imaginatively improve the lines in the North.

Representation

One opportunity is to do representative things, keeping the flag flying for the North. This is not an easy task when the centres of power in Glasgow and Edinburgh are over 300 miles away from Wick and Thurso and more than 150 miles away even from Inverness. Even more so when the big chiefs frequently scheduled morning meetings early, forgetting that the first train from Inverness did not get south before 10 am.

Getting policy statements drawn up for FoFNL's aims was my first priority. These covered line capacity and speed; rolling stock; and service timings and frequency; and were worked on from 1994 onwards.

Publicising and explaining our views was the next stage. Grounded in the newsletters and on the website, influential people still had to be made aware of our existence and views.

A paper was given to a joint meeting of railway promotion groups in Glasgow organised by the Rail Passengers Committee for Scotland (RPCS) and chaired by their Vice-Convener, James King, on 28 February 2004. This got our ideas for the north over to representatives from the whole of Scotland and was summarised in the May 2004 issue [no 31] of the Newsletter.

Another paper was given at the last ever meeting of the RPCS with Mike Lunan, their Convener, in charge and which happened to be held in Dingwall in May 2005. We didn't know it at the time but it turned out to be a primer for his taking over the reins at FoFNL!

I took our paper about a new train for long distance rural routes to national meetings of the Association of Community Rail Partnerships in Darlington and Crewe. We didn't really manage to get the likes of the Settle and Carlisle or Cambrian Coast line groups properly engaged with this and in the 2020s we will still be waiting for a suitable tailor-made new train for the FNL and others. Meanwhile, the class 158s soldier on.

Winter Meetings and Summer Outings

These were started with some success, although the numbers attending were always small. Twenty was a really good turnout. Syd Atkinson, who had been Area Manager at Inverness, was an extremely good raconteur and held us spellbound when talking about operating matters and particularly the terrible winter storm of 1978.

Photo: Richard Ardern

The summer excursions were fun too. The idea was to visit the lesser used stations. We went gold panning at Kildonan, tutored by the local postman; and visited the RSPB reserve at Forsinard; and Dunrobin Castle where most of the party walked back along the shore to catch the train south from Golspie.

It was sometimes difficult to make the outings work for members from both ends of the line. Forsinard was easy because most of the trains crossed there. The last challenge was only a few years ago with a visit from Thurso to Altnabreac led by our President, John Thurso, who shared his boyhood memories of being allowed to help at the station and to work the signals. Lewis Sinclair also joined us en route at Scotscalder and told us about his work with the permanent way gang on the northern section. We were only at Altnabreac for 20 minutes The timetable alternative of nearly four hours would have taxed everybody's resilience due to the midges!

Service Deceleration and the Start of the Long, Long Road to Recovery

2005 was a pivotal year in the fortunes of the FNL. Frank Roach at the Highland Rail Partnership had followed on the success of the Beauly station reopening with the "Invernet" plans. This was a considerable expansion in the number of trains serving the Inverness commuting area from and to Easter Ross. The timetable had been drawn up but a hiatus with the Strategic Rail Authority led to a year's delay in finalising the funding package. Other events further south led to the national roll-out of safety improvements, principally TPWS (Train Protection Warning System): the blue flashing lights at the end of each loop.

This caused the bombshell of significant deceleration of FNL services which led to an eventual total of 25 minutes being added to the total journey time between Wick and Inverness. (We had originally been warned to expect an 8 minute end to end deceleration). Timings for the Invernet services introduced in December 2005 were badly affected too.

This journey time setback has led to all sorts of difficulties in scheduling trains on the line to cope with the single track and the sparsity of loops. In particular it made the 1988 decision to close the Lentran loop critical to the successful operation of the line.

Highland Rail Partnership

Succeeding John Melling as the representative for all three Friends groups (Far North, Kyle and West Highland Lines in alphabetical order) was challenging, but having lived in Helensburgh I did have some knowledge of the West Highland lines too. As an amateur I was constantly learning how things were done on the railway and what would be difficult to do.

After a few years, I was asked to become a full Director of the HRP, registering with Companies House, and helping to support Frank Roach and Chris Kendall the two employees who worked from the Lairg Station office. Indeed, when they eventually became employees of HITRANS, I was one of the two remaining directors entrusted with winding up the company.

One of the most interesting activities at HRP was an initiative to try to get a steam train running on the FNL which would provide an outing for cruise passengers from Invergordon and also attract steam enthusiasts. We had meetings with John Cameron, the owner of *The Great Marquess* locomotive, and with James Shuttleworth who had masterminded the Jacobite steam service between Fort William and Mallaig. We investigated both Helmsdale and Brora as destinations from which to reverse the train. Finding paths on such a long line with so few loops was only one of the difficulties and, sadly, our aims were not realised.

FoFNL Lobbying

Lobbying has perhaps been the most important role of FoFNL. Lobbying for money to be spent on our line and on the two umbilical cords which connect us to the rest of the passenger and freight network through Perth and Aberdeen. Everything seems to take so long to achieve, that it would be easy to become depressed, except for the belief that what we are trying to achieve is worthwhile.

FoFNL owes a great deal of gratitude to so many railway people and to the wider family from planners to politicians, and to two in particular, John Yellowlees and Frank Roach. Our story, enriched by the many talented individuals among our membership, can be followed through the years on the pages of the *Far North Express*.

Richard Ardern

Gavin Sinclair joined FoFNL in 1997 and was our Secretary from 2005 to 2014. Originally from Watten, near Wick, he now lives in London. He is involved in Management Consultancy and specialises in rail business planning. FoFNL frequently calls upon Gavin's skills and knowledge to help unravel difficult questions.

FAR NORTH TIMETABLE EVOLUTION

This review of the Far North Line timetable describes changes to the weekday (Monday to Saturday) timetable since the formation of Friends of the Far North Line in 1994, through to the present day. Sunday services are also described but only where there have been significant changes.

From the introduction of Class 156 'Super Sprinter' units on the Far North Line in 1989, the established timetable was three trains each way between Inverness and Thurso/Wick. Trains operated between Inverness and Thurso with a connection at Georgemas Junction for Wick – with one exception where Wick had a through working to Inverness to return the unit back to Inverness for fuel and maintenance. Trains departed Inverness at 07:12, 11:00 and at 18:00. From Thurso, trains departed at 06:08 (connection from Wick at 06:00), 11:32 (11:24) and at 15:42 (to Georgemas Junction with the Inverness train departing Wick at 15:34). A mid-afternoon Inverness to Tain train operated in the winter and extended to Wick and Thurso in the summer timetable. In the winter timetable, the return working arrived back in Inverness at 17:45; in the summer this did not run and instead the summer only late evening from Thurso at 20:00 operated (with a connection from Wick at 19:52). In the summer, when trains were strengthened to 4-cars, trains would divide at Georgemas Junction with a portion to each of Thurso and Wick.

The May 1994 timetable retained this fourth summer-only service between Inverness and Wick. The main change from previous years, however, was to bring forward the summer evening service, departing from Wick at 17:20 and running via Thurso (depart 17:57), providing an earlier arrival in Inverness at 21:45. The summer-only northbound train at 15:48 from Inverness also operated via Thurso, arriving in Wick at 20:07.

Sunday services only operated in the summer timetable, with two trains each way between Inverness and Thurso/Wick. In 1994 the service was slightly reduced with the Inverness to Brora mid-afternoon return service withdrawn, which in previous years provided a third pair of services north of Inverness. The last train from Inverness to the north was brought forward to depart Inverness two hours earlier at 14:40. Trains operated between Inverness and Thurso with connections to and from Wick.

The winter 1994/95 timetable returned to the usual pattern of three trains between Inverness and Thurso/Wick with the mid-afternoon service between Inverness and Tain retained.

The timetable introduced in May 1995 saw considerable change to the Far North Line. The timetable retained three trains per day each way between Inverness and Wick (instead of the usual four in the summer timetable) and all trains operated via Thurso with the train crew depot there closing. This resulted in journey times between Inverness and Wick being extended by an average of 27 minutes, with a best journey time of 4 hours 15 minutes. The last train from Inverness to Wick departed considerably earlier at 16:45 which reduced journey opportunities, with fewer connections available beyond Inverness. The mid-afternoon Inverness to Tain return services was withdrawn. The Sunday level of service of two trains each way was retained but with Wick trains operating via Thurso.

The winter timetable introduced in September 1995 improved connectivity from the south by the retiming of the last train from Inverness to Wick 30 minutes later at 17:15, thereby connecting out of the 13:40 from Edinburgh. A small journey time improvement of 5 minutes between Inverness and Wick was achieved.

The summer timetable introduced in June 1996 made use of the additional rolling stock that provided additional capacity in the summer months. One unit that would otherwise strengthen trains to 4-cars was instead used to provide a connection and portion working at Georgemas Junction – the first train from Inverness to Thurso had a connection to Wick and the midday train from Wick was a portion, combining with the Thurso portion at Georgemas Junction, therefore reducing journey times to and from Wick.

In the 1998 and 1999 summer timetables the 06:00 from Wick and 11:05 from Inverness were reduced from 4- to 2-cars.

In March 1998 the first steps were made to provide a commuting service into Inverness from the south end of the line and an additional morning service was introduced on Mondays to Fridays from Dingwall at 08:00, arriving in Inverness at 08:25. The 17:15 Inverness to Wick provided the corresponding evening return train home for commuters.

The summer 2000 timetable saw significant positive changes with the introduction of Class 158 'Express' units on the Far North Line. Three trains were provided in each direction; all trains were formed of 2-cars, so the previous summer arrangements of connection and portion working for Wick were withdrawn and all trains operated between Inverness and Wick via Thurso. The Class 158 units enabled journey times to be reduced by 18 minutes on average. The number of bicycle spaces was reduced from six to two per 2-car unit. In the summer months, bicycles were conveyed by road transport between Inverness and Wick. This arrangement was withdrawn when the Class 158s were refurbished to accommodate additional bicycle space and with the introduction of additional train services in 2008.

The introduction of Class 158 units on the Far North and Kyle lines allowed trains to operate across Inverness – the 06:32 from Wick operated through to Edinburgh (arrive 14:03) and the 17:30 from Inverness to Wick was a through train from Edinburgh (depart 13:40). As Class 170 'Turbostars' were introduced between Inverness, Edinburgh and Glasgow, this arrangement was gradually withdrawn.

From September 2001, Sunday services were provided all year round rather than just for the summer months. For the winter period between September and May, one train was provided in each direction – 13:40 from Wick and 18:30 from Inverness. In the summer, a second train was provided as in previous years. From May 2002 the 13:40 from Wick was retimed approximately two hours earlier to improve connections at Inverness for the south.

In May 2001 the morning Dingwall commuter train was extended to start back from Tain. Initially, this operated on Mondays to Fridays; from the May 2003 timetable change, this train ran on Saturdays too.

Beauly station re-opened in 2002 with all trains calling there for the first time since 1960.

In 2004 and 2005 performance on the Far North Line deteriorated significantly owing to a number of operational problems including speed restrictions; this meant the Sectional Running Times (SRTs) – the time taken to travel between each station – were unachievable. This meant that trains often ran late and frequently missed out Thurso to save time on their way to and from Wick. The June 2005 timetable addressed these problems by correcting the SRTs; this led to end-to-end journey times increasing by 20 minutes, removing the journey time improvements introduced in May 2000. The timetable also had to be restructured to accommodate the longer journey times:

- the second train of the day at 11:27 from Inverness to Wick was brought forward to depart Inverness at 10:39; and

- the second train of the day from Wick was retimed 30 minutes later, arriving in Inverness at 16:49.

June 2005 also saw the introduction of the first phase of substantial train service improvements delivered as 'Invernet' which extended commuting opportunities from further north and improved off-peak frequencies. These included:

- extending the Tain to Inverness morning commuter train to start back from Lairg at 06:33;

- additional services from Inverness during the day to Invergordon and Tain;

- a new evening peak departure from Inverness at 17:03 to Ardgay; and

- a new late evening service from Inverness at 20:39 to Tain.

This was supplemented in December 2006 with a fourth train from Wick to Inverness. Departing Wick at 08:13, it had a journey time of 4 hours to Inverness and connected out of the of the early morning ferry crossing from Stromness.

The December 2008 timetable included a third tranche of train service improvements:

- a new early train from Ardgay to Inverness, arriving at 07:44 providing a connection into the 07:55 departure from Inverness to London King's Cross;

- a fourth northbound train from Inverness to Wick at 13:56, filling the seven-hour gap between services and connecting with the evening ferry from Scrabster to Stromness; and

- a new late service from Inverness at 23:30 to Tain, which operated on Friday and Saturday evenings.

The first train from Kyle of Lochalsh to Inverness was retimed earlier; this meant that passengers from Dingwall, Muir of Ord and Beauly now had three services arriving in Inverness between 07:45 and 09:00.

The Sunday service was improved overall, with additional all-year services operating between Inverness and Tain throughout the day. Consequently, the summer-only two trains between Inverness and Wick was reduced to one – departing Wick at midday and returning from Inverness at 18:00.

Since 2008, some modest changes have been introduced, most of these involving minor re-timing to improve punctuality. Significantly, in December 2016, the last train from Inverness to Wick was retimed 30 minutes later (as a consequence of the early afternoon train from Wick being slowed down and arriving in Inverness later). This meant, however, that connections were available from Glasgow as late as 15:09 and at 10:00 from London King's Cross. It also meant that there were three evening peak departures from Inverness to Dingwall between 17:00 and 18:30.

Conon Bridge station re-opened in 2013 with trains calling here for the first time since 1960. Most trains between Inverness, Kyle of Lochalsh and Wick call at Conon Bridge, with a journey time of 28 minutes from Inverness.

When Class 158s were introduced in May 2000, the average journey time between Inverness and Wick was 3 hours 50 minutes. By 2018, this had increased to 4 hours 21 minutes. The reasons for this include:

- two new stations on the Far North Line at Beauly and Conon Bridge;

- double the number of trains operating which means more time to allow trains to pass each other;

- more trains making booked stops at stations, rather than on request only, for example at Alness and at Fearn;

- the timetable allowing for all speed restrictions entering and leaving loops at stations and at level crossings, improving performance; and

- additional time for RETB token exchanges.

Gavin Sinclair

FoFNL's Treasurer is **David Start**. He took over from Janice Stewart in the summer of 2008.

David was born and educated in Worthing in Sussex, where he still lives, and has had a varied career in the Post Office, shipping, retail sector, and publishing. He is a keen book collector, photographer and passionate cricket enthusiast! He also works for the local community and volunteers for the Air Ambulance.

Having been a regular traveller to Scotland for many years, David joined FoFNL after meeting Charles Kennedy MP when the sleeper service was under threat.

Iain MacDonald had a 50 year long career as a railway signalman on the Highland rail lines. He was one of the pioneer operators of the Radio Electronic Token Block system until his retirement. He was known to his fellow railwaymen as "The Blackbird" due to his cheerful whistling. He has been a committee member of FoFNL since 2005 and mails out each issue of the magazine.

This article by Iain, published in the June 2007 edition of the FoFNL Newsletter, is an example of the detailed knowledge that he has brought to us.

An insight into the technicalities involved with the introduction of a chord at Georgemas

For many years it has been an aspiration of FoFNL to have a chord built at Georgemas to allow direct running to Thurso with only one reversal necessary to reach Wick. Following on from various conversations with former signalman Iain MacDonald, your Editor invited him to submit a description of the equipment and techniques required to achieve the chord.

After the acquisition of land and track two new junction type points layouts would need to be created. When trains are approaching points where the lines diverge they are referred to as "facing points" and when approaching points where lines meet they are called "trailing points" and each direction of traversing the points requires a different set of equipment and procedure.

When approaching from a trailing direction the track circuit is activated for the line concerned and the points move to the correct position and the relevant points set indicator (psi) is illuminated. If this procedure fails the driver stops at the unlit psi and on the signallers instructions walks to the plunger and attempts to set the route, and if that fails a points operator is required. Unlike hydraulic points, which the train wheels push aside, a driver is not allowed to clamp and scotch these points as they have motors.

When a train approaches in the facing direction the points mechanism has no way of knowing in which direction the train wishes to travel and this is why clamp lock points are required and route selection is made by applying the left or right hand plunger; this being the same way as a route is set up in a signalbox by the signaller. Unfortunately this can not be done remotely but entails the driver having to stop, leave his cab and operate the appropriate plunger as is done presently at Dingwall and Georgemas.

Trains are not allowed to stop within the controlling treadles and track circuits of an AOCL (Automatic Open Crossing Locally Monitored) level crossing as this will fail the crossing and cause problems. As there is an AOCL at Halkirk care will have to be taken when locating the stop board and the points leading onto the chord.

Iain MacDonald

PSI when approaching from Georgemas

Halkirk Junction points.
A similar arrangement will be required where the new line would join the existing Georgemas to Thurso line

Points motor

Stop board

Route indicators and PSI
Left theatre would show B for branch and right theatre would show M for main line

Driver's plunger

PSI when approaching from Thurso

22

Mike Lunan, an actuary by profession was, until its abolition in 2005, Convener of the Rail Passengers' Committee for Scotland. He has been FoFNL Convener for two separate periods - 2005-9 and 2015-18. With his turn of phrase and uncompromising clarity on FoFNL's aims he is highly respected by the Scottish rail industry.

A Convener Looks Back...

When I was first elected as Convener in late 2005 FoFNL was a bitterly divided body. A small group - perhaps 25% of the membership - supported the construction of a rail bridge paralleling the road bridge over the Dornoch Firth. The bulk of the membership agreed with me that while such a bridge would be nice to have, the cost of construction was woefully unrealistic. The election was contested: pro- and anti-Dornoch Bridge. The losers, unwilling to accept defeat graciously, largely resigned or failed to renew. While this meant that FoFNL's numbers were fewer its voice was strengthened: it spoke sense to the railway industry, and it did so with one voice.

Few of the advances that FoFNL has helped to bring about since then are likely to have been achieved without this clear-headed unity: the fourth train each day running end to end; better Invernet services; the equipping of the Class 158s with retention toilets; the re-opening of Beauly and Conon Bridge stations; the setting-up of Transport Scotland's Review Team. FoFNL is now a respected stakeholder within the tent that is the Scottish railway industry, and the successive line-ups of guest speakers at our Annual Conference is testimony to that. There can be few Rail User Groups who can attract the Chief Executive of Network Rail, the Cabinet Secretary with overall responsibility for railways, the senior Civil Servant through whom his decisions are transmitted for action, successive Managing Directors of ScotRail. And being so far from the Central Belt, visiting us for our Conference gives these gentlemen (and one lady) the chance to see a bit of Scotland that other beers don't reach.

As I write on Day 32 of CP6 the future looks rosy. Network Rail has put a lot of work into studying what needs to be done to improve the service of the Far North Line - things big and small, like re-laying a lot of line and mending some fences - and an announcement about long-term infrastructure enhancements is keenly awaited. The Far North Line has come a long way in the last 15 years: will my successors look back in 2034 and marvel at what was achieved in the next 15?

Mike Lunan

Bob Barnes-Watts or 'BBW' was one of FoFNL's leading lights during his time on the committee. His untimely death in 2018 has deprived the organisation of a huge fund of knowledge, experience and expertise.

At the time of his death he was still working in the rail industry on a freelance basis and was often able to give us advance warning of approaching catastrophes such as the timetable meltdown in 2018.

During early discussions about the format of this publication Bob fortunately put fingers to keyboard and wrote down his thoughts and suggestions:

25th Anniversary Booklet

Friends of the Far North Line exists because we are the campaign group for rail north of Inverness - lobbying for improved services for the local user, tourist and freight operator.

Actually FoFNL realises that the line does not exist in splendid isolation, hence the enormous effort expended over the past 24 years in reminding those in control of both the purse and policy strings of their responsibility to continue the improvements to the routes feeding the North Highland Lines as a whole.

To most people, a train is a utility, something to be used to get to a place of work, recreation and the like; to others a journey is an end in itself.

23

However the measure by which the success to both categories of traveller is taken is by seeing what is on offer to a potential user.

When I became involved with FoFNL in 2005/06, thanks to John Yellowlees and Frank Roach, FoFNL was experiencing some personality clashes and differing views on what should happen in the future. Despite that, there was a buzz about the place with Invernet close to implementation ... exciting times for us but, more importantly, the passengers, both existing and those who would in future choose rail over other modes.

In November 2008, Callum MacLeod who was the Business Manager, Highland, based in Inverness from 1986-1991, came up from Swindon to give a talk at the FoFNL Winter Meeting. At dinner that evening I handed him a copy of the NHL timetable for December. On looking at what was on offer, he said, "My boy, this level of service was but a distant dream in my time here".

The dreams were turned into reality thanks to various entities and by the tireless support of the Friends. We also had (and still have) our own ideas and many were adopted.

To my mind the best way to see what has been accomplished since 1994 is to simply look at both the timetables and the 'Editorial/Headcode' pieces featured in each newsletter/*FNE*.

In September 1994 there were 7 arrivals at Inverness from the North Highlands Lines between 09:39 and 19:48; there are now 14, the first at 07:43, the last at 23:31.

Currently there are 12 trains leaving Inverness between 07:00 and 21:07 with a 13th on Fridays and Saturdays at 23:33.

Also we shouldn't forget the Midnight To Muir at the weekend, a train linking cities that never sleep. OK, tongue out of cheek, but it does satisfy the Abellio promise to help the burgeoning night time economy of Scotland.

[BBW]

John Brandon held the post of Convener from July 2009 until May 2014. John is a professional railwayman and is a Member of the Institution of Railway Operators. His no-nonsense style is exemplified in this FoFNL AGM Report.

Convener's Report For The 2011 FoFNL AGM

The past year has seen a number of successes in our campaigning for improvements to train services on the Far North Line. The portions of the 17:52 from Inverness were reversed so that the Wick section is on the front, thus shortening journey times for the majority of passengers, and we have succeeded in having stops by trains at Dunrobin Castle aligned with the opening dates and hours of the Castle. This, we understand, is the most popular tourist attraction north of the Great Glen with some 50 000 visitors a year, and these timetable changes, along with an advertising campaign by the Castle, which stresses the convenience of using rail and gives a discount on entry to rail passengers, will, we hope, have a very beneficial effect upon rail use at the northern end of our line. Many thanks to Bob Barnes-Watts for his work on this. Unfortunately, we have lost one of our rail-served attractions for the time being. During the bad weather last winter, part of the roof of Carbisdale Castle, now a Youth Hostel and served by Culrain station, collapsed under the weight of snow and it has been closed since. We understand that it is proposed to reopen it in September but we will, of course, have lost the summer season.

We still have some way to go: a "wish-list" of improvements to the Far North Line and to connectivity from both Aberdeen and via the Highland Main Line was published in the most recent newsletter. We remain concerned at the six-hour gap in services to Inverness from Alness, Ross and Cromarty's largest town, and we will continue to campaign for the 08:12 from Wick to call there. The saga of Conon Bridge station limps towards its hopeful conclusion of reopening but progress has been slow.

The line suffered quite badly during the first bout of bad weather experienced last winter. Much of this has been covered in the newsletters but it seems that the railway authorities in remote Glasgow may have misunderstood the situation in the north of Scotland. I'm pleased to say that, when the weather deteriorated again, the effect was less.

Members will recall that, in my report last year, I mentioned the informal gathering which the Secretary and I had attended at Portcullis House and that some interesting developments had come from that. You will have read in subsequent newsletters that these pertained to proposals for an hourly train service between Inverness and Tain and that, subsequently, I attended a meeting in Glasgow with Transport Scotland (TS) and HITRANS at which these were tabled. They were received favourably and we were led to believe that TS would be taking them forward to produce a business case. However, the eventual response we received was that, because we hadn't done the business case, they could not be taken forward. HITRANS also advised us that they were unable to arrange it. This left us in somewhat of a "Catch 22" situation. I am, however, pleased to be able to report that we have received an offer for the business case to be produced at a reduced rate and we are currently investigating how this could be financed. Sadly, even this reduced rate is beyond HITRANS.

Committee members have, once again, been active in representing the society at numerous meetings and have put in a great deal of time and effort on our behalf. An organisation such as the Friends of the Far North Line could not function without the input of all of the committee and I thank them for the hard work they've all done over the past year.

John Brandon

FoFNL has several connections with music: Mike Lunan has sung under many great conductors, especially as a past member of the Edinburgh Festival Chorus; Ian Budd was an orchestral player for over forty years; the late Bob Barnes-Watts, our travel connections and timetable guru, was a radio DJ in the States for 17 years and **Malcolm Wood** graduated from the Royal Manchester College of Music as a solo singer and pianist before becoming a music teacher.

Malcolm, one of our committee members and Secretary from 2014-9 now performs one of FoFNL's most useful functions.

Having become exasperated by the shocking punctuality, or lack of it, on the line, in 2016 he offered to compile and maintain spreadsheets of weekly performance.

It seems likely that the fact that the railway runs at the bottom of his garden made him extra-aware of trains going past at all the wrong times!

Although ScotRail and Network Rail obviously keep records of all train movements it is extremely useful to FoFNL to be able to watch trends and pick up on specific instances every week.

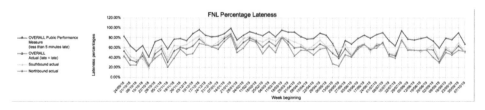

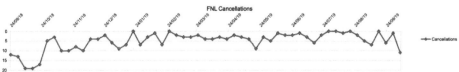

Continued - P28

47787 at Dingwall with Royal Scotsman on 5 May 2009

SANDY COLLEY
FoFNL's Most Prolific Photographer

FoFNL member and ex-committee member, Sandy, has an eye for a beautiful setting.

ScotRail 'Classic' HST approaching Inverness on the HML, 26 July 2018

[Left] **British Railways 2-6-0 78052 at Dornoch July 1957.**

[Centre left] **As things looked at Thurso in 1995.**

[Centre right] **66111 with Lairg tanks at Clachnaharry, 9 June 2005.**

[Bottom] **67007 with Lairg tanks at Fearn, 6 November 2010.**

Week beginning: 16-09-2019

FAR NORTH LINE - Southbound

Train	Due at Inverness	Minutes late at Inverness:					
		Monday	Tuesday	Wednesday	Thursday	Friday	Saturday
0614 ex Ardgay	0743	RT	RT	RT	RT	2E	1E
0626 ex Lairg	0812	1E	RT	1E	RT	1E	RT
0618 ex Wick	1035	RT	8L	7L	1L	2E	1E
0802 ex Wick	1226	1L	1L	4L	1E ^^	RT	RT
1551 ex Invergordon	1646	5L	RT	RT	2E	4L	RT
1234 ex Wick	1702	6L	1E	2E	1E	2L	1E
1600 ex Wick	2010	RT	2E	RT	1E	6L	RT
1928 ex Ardgay	2057	RT	RT	8L	1L	3L	1E
2221 ex Tain	2331	4L	7L	34L	1L	21L	2L
0048 ex Tain FSO	To Muir of Ord 0131a	n/a	n/a	n/a	n/a	20L	2L

^^ no trolley.

OVERALL WEEKLY PERFORMANCE:	**56%** on time or early.	(**60.7%** Southbound - **50%** Northbound)		**nil** CANCELLATIONS

OVERALL ON TIME OR LESS THAN 5 MINUTES LATE AT DESTINATION :	**79%**

FAR NORTH LINE - Northbound

Departing Inverness at:	Destination:	Due at destination:	Minutes late at destination:					
			Monday	Tuesday	Wednesday	Thursday	Friday	Saturday
0700	Wick	1131	RT	1E	19L	10L	RT	RT
1041	Wick	1456	7L	1E	4L	4L	4L	4L
1400	Wick	1822	RT	RT	1E	1E ^^	8L	RT
1450	Invergordon	1541	2L	RT	RT	RT	3L	RT
1712	Ardgay	1839	RT	1L	13L	3L	RT	RT
1831	Wick	2252	10L	1E	2E	RT	1E	RT
2106	Tain	2216	6L	9L	31L	1L	19L	2L
2333 FSO	Tain	0043	n/a	n/a	n/a	n/a	23L	4L
Caledonian Sleeper from Euston	(due Inverness 0839)		RT	2E	1L	RT	3E	6E
Highland Chieftain from Kings Cross	(due Inverness 2004)		28L	5L	5L	2L	5L	59L

^^ no trolley.

M.G.W. 22-09-2019

Malcolm's tables and graphs are available at www.fofnl.org/archives/lateness/index.php

TIMELINE

Before embarking upon this survey of FoFNL's 25 years here are a couple of items predating FoFNL.

Long before our formation there were stirrings of interest in openings, not closings. This news item was in the March 1961 *Railway Magazine*:

TRAIN SERVICES IN NORTHERN SCOTLAND

Rogart station is to be reopened but the continuance of the restored railway facilities will be dependent on adequate patronage.

It may be hoped that a similar decision will be taken in other cases. Halkirk and Muir of Ord are two places that come readily to mind; both are of fair size and had conveniently situated stations.

Rogart was the first of the 1960 major raft of closures to be reversed, having been closed for only nine months. Muir of Ord was eventually reopened in 1976, due to the efforts of Councillor (and former FoFNL member) David Martin. Halkirk (in conjunction with a Georgemas Chord) is on FoFNL's wish list.

David Martin is pictured in June 2012 having just unveiled the plaque celebrating the 150th Anniversary of the opening of the railway to Muir of Ord.

Photo: John Yellowlees

ARGUING YOUR CASE

There's more than one way to promote a railway. This is "MacPuff", the mascot of the first campaign group for the Far North Line, in 1963, known as *The Highland Vigilantes*.

There is a direct link between MacPuff and FoFNL - Donald MacCuish, who was for 25 years Transport Officer of the Highlands and Islands Development Board - was, prior to that, a member of the Highland Transport Committee, set up to oppose the Beeching cuts in the Highlands, from which sprang the "Vigilantes". He joined the FoFNL Committee in 2000.

MacPuff car badge, designed by Donald Shearer.
Photo: Alasdair Cameron

DORNOCH BRIDGE

The line was saved in 1964, but the subsequent road bridges across the three firths became a further major threat to the railway and construction of a much shorter and more direct rail line between Tain and Golspie across the Dornoch Firth was requested and very nearly achieved.

Following on from the refusal of the Scottish Office to plug the estimated £4m funding gap for the direct rail link, the Highland Council and HIDB commissioned economic consultant Tony Mackay in October 1986 to conduct a very rapid study of "additional and significant wider social and economic benefits which had not featured in the narrower financial appraisal". The Scottish Office challenged Mackay's findings and stood by their rejection. They subsequently explained their reasons to Sir Russell Johnston MP. Thereafter, this letter to him from ScotRail finally drew the curtains on the issue.

J.S. Cornell: *General Manager*

V.A. Chadwick: *Deputy General Manager*

 **ScotRail**

ScotRail House, 58 Port Dundas Road, Glasgow G4 0HG   Telephone: 041-332 9811 ext. 3252 Telex: 299431

24 July, 1986.

Sir Russell Johnston, MP.,
House of Commons,
LONDON SW1A OAA.

Dear Sir Russell,

　　　　Thank you for your letter and I can understand your concern for the present situation.

　　　　As you are aware, we have made it clear that without external financial help there is no way that B.R. can take the project forward as it does not meet investment criteria.

　　　　The Scottish Office have also made it very clear to the Board that they cannot put money into the rail part of the project as it is not an economic case.

　　　　We are, however, continuing with our efforts for the wellbeing of the North Line and are looking at ways of promoting the line, decreasing journey times and introducing Sprinter trains in 1988.

　　　　I am certainly not regarding the loss of a rail link at this time as saying goodbye to the line.

Regards,

Jim Cornell.

COLLAPSE OF THE RIVER NESS RAIL BRIDGE

I was General Manager of British Rail's ScotRail division from September, 1987 until January, 1990. On 6th February, 1989 I travelled to Inverness for a meeting with Highland Regional Council the following day. There had been a huge amount of rain in the north and I was told that the River Ness was in full spate. In the evening I went down to the river and it was lapping the embankments and running at a fearsome rate. The Ness has the steepest fall of any river in the country, and it was certainly evident.

Photo: Courtesy of Network Rail

The following morning I was having breakfast in the hotel (porridge and kippers of course!) when an ashen-faced Ronnie Munro, the Station Manager, came in to tell us that the railway bridge had been washed away. When I went down to look, the rails were suspended above the raging river, with no sign of the bridge spans.

There was obviously great concern locally that the bridge would not be replaced. I had a hectic morning of telephone calls with British Railways Board Headquarters and many others, and was able to get a verbal agreement that the bridge would be replaced. I therefore arranged a press conference that afternoon to make this announcement. This was to ensure that there were no second thoughts at Board HQ, in the Other Provincial Services business sector, or in the Department of Transport!

Then followed all of the decisions, debates and arguments about what we should do about train services to the Far North and Kyle of Lochalsh, what the design of the bridge should be, and how to deal with a claim for damages from the Harbour Board owing to the debris from the bridge blocking the harbour!

It was agreed to operate a shuttle service with a bus connection from Inverness. There was a diesel multiple unit trapped north of the bridge, but more units had to be transported by road to provide the temporary fleet. A temporary maintenance depot was created at Muir of Ord using a converted civil engineering shed.

It was eventually agreed to replace the bridge with a modern steel structure. Rail services were restored in 1990.

John Ellis

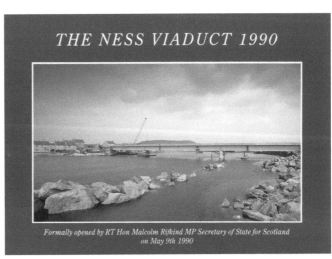

THE NESS VIADUCT 1990

Formally opened by RT Hon Malcolm Rifkind MP Secretary of State for Scotland on May 9th 1990

FoFNL Conference 1995

The conference on 26 October 1995 concerned the future of the Far North Line and was organised by the then FoFNL Secretary, Frank Roach.

The event was extremely successful and from it sprang the Highland Rail Network Development Partnership bringing together local authorities and the rail industry. This group was eventually subsumed into the Highlands and Islands Transport Partnership, HITRANS, for whom Frank holds the position of Partnership Manager Responsible for Rail on the Executive team. A report of the conference by John Allison of the Highland Railway Society was published in their journal in 1996 and is reproduced here. Although much has been achieved since 1995 some of the fundamental problems of the Far North Line remain and still feature very prominently.

Conference on the Future of the Far North Line

While much doom and gloom surrounds the 'privatisation' of British Rail it was extremely heartening to spend a day discussing, in a very positive way, the future development of one of Britain's most scenic routes - the Far North Line.

Speakers at the conference included Robert Maclennan MP, President of the Friends of the Far North Line, Julian Worth, Transrail, and John Ellis, ScotRail. Brian Wilson MP, Shadow Spokesman on Transport, was also due to speak but unfortunately Parliamentary business prevented him from attending. Such was the importance he attached to the conference that his speech was delivered on his behalf by conference organiser Frank Roach, Secretary of the Friends of the Far North Line. Frank is due. and on the day received. much praise for drawing together nearly 120 people who have an interest in the railways in the Highlands and the Far North Line in particular and for establishing a most impressive list of speakers.

Some of the key commitments given were as follows :

ScotRail proposes to introduce, in the next summer's timetable and earlier if possible, a commuter train leaving Tain at approximately 07:30 and arriving in Inverness at around 08:30 using an existing two car Class 156 unit between turns. With the last train north now returned to a 17:15 departure from Inverness it will, for the first time for many years, be possible to commute to Inverness by train for people living in the rapidly expanding travel to work area for Inverness. ScotRail will attempt to achieve a three hour journey time from Wick to Inverness by a programme of running line improvements and a careful inspection of speed limits on the line. Many of the speed limits have not been reassessed since the introduction of Sprinter stock and still apply to locomotive hauled trains. This proposal will require considerable capital investment and ScotRail is looking for partners to contribute. Highlands & Islands Enterprise (the replacement for the Highlands & Islands Development Board) immediately committed themselves to 50% of the cost of an estimated £25,000 engineering survey of the line.

Julian Worth of Transrail referred to the success of the first freight train for 15 years on the line. This had carried rolled steel for Norfrost Freezers and domestic coal north and had returned with scrap metal and manufactured freezer cabinets for export to America. The next train is due on 9 November with a similar load but will drop off wagons at Lairg to be loaded with marble from Ledmore quarry. This will be picked up by the returning train the following day. The marble is of world class quality and is bound, via the Channel Tunnel, for Italy for cutting and finishing. Apparently the skills to finish the stone do not exist, at present, in this country but it is hoped these will be developed. The manager of the quarry indicated that Transrail was the only method of transport which could get the stone to Italy at an economic cost to compete with Italian Carrera marble and hoped that his quarry was setting an example to others.

The second freight train on 9 November will experimentally carry a wagon loaded with 30 metre steel pipes for the Rockwater Pipe yard north of Wick. At present the pipes are carried by road and are the bane of all motorists especially on the Berriedale Braes north of Helmsdale where they have become stuck.

31

Transrail is negotiating with Railtrack to stop freight trains overnight on the running line to allow timber to be loaded direct from the line side forests and therefore cutting out transshipment costs.

John Ellis of ScotRail explained that ScotRail had no intention of taking any steps to resurrect the Dornoch Firth Rail Crossing because of the need to persuade Railtrack, among others, to make the investment. He was convinced that for a great deal less investment many other improvements could be made to the line. These would help to achieve the ultimate aim of a three hour journey time while at the same time preserving the Lairg loop. This is a vital source of passengers and potential freight traffic which could help to spread the rail access costs over a larger number of trains. Although there were murmurings of disappointment from some members of the audience, the vast majority accepted that the window of opportunity for the Dornoch Firth rail crossing has passed.

Railtrack confirmed their wish to undertake an engineering survey of the line to ensure it remained available for use by passenger and freight trains and to determine what was required to increase line speeds and welcomed the ScotRail and H&IE commitment to this project.

The final contribution to the conference came from Andrew Seedhouse based at Plymouth University, who has successfully created a partnership to promote branch lines in Devon and who has gained support for these activities from ERDF funds. The audience was most impressed with Mr Seedhouse's presentation and he, in turn, was most impressed with ScotRail's positive attitude to the development of the Highland rail network. From his presentation it seemed that Regional Railways in England were only interested in the main trunk routes rather than minor routes or branch lines.

Dr Ken MacTaggart of Highlands & Islands Enterprise offered to hold a meeting of interested parties to attempt to establish a similar partnership and to see what steps could be taken to integrate the transport network perhaps by the establishment of a PTA as suggested by Brian Wilson, to examine the development and promotion of all the railways in the Highlands, and to look closely at appointing a Railways Development Officer.

The conference concluded with a question and answer session.

John Allison

March 1998 - the start of commuter services. Arguably this was one of the greatest milestones in the change in attitude towards the line. From here on it has been obvious that the removal of the six mile double-track section of the line between Clachnaharry and Clunes in 1966 and replacement with a loop at Lentran was unfortunate. The removal of that loop in 1988 has made it extremely difficult to keep to the timetable.

Newsletter - February 1998

SCOTRAIL'S £1 TRAIN TRIP FOR DINGWALL DENIZENS

So runs the headline for the latest press release issued by ScotRail on 5th February.

The details were announced by ScotRail's Managing Director, Alastair McPherson at the meeting of the Highland Rail Network Development Partnership in Inverness.

The plan is to run the service from Dingwall at 08.00, calling at Muir of Ord at 08.05 and reaching Inverness at 08.25. Commuters will be able to return on existing trains at 17.15 and 18.00.

An introductory £10 flexipass, valid, for a month, for ten single journeys in either direction on any service between Dingwall or Muir of Ord and Inverness, will be in place for the launch of the new service on March 2nd for a four month trial period.

"This is the first of a number of new services ScotRail plan to introduce. It is our response to a specific request from Highland Council who in recent years have become increasingly concerned about road congestion in Inverness, particularly in the morning peak. It demonstrates the very positive working relationship that we have with them and with other members of the Partnership." Then Mr. McPherson gave a warning - 'use it or lose it'.

The Friends of the Far North Line has been pressing for a commuter train from Tain for four years and we welcome this as a start. The Highland Rail Network Development Partnership was founded following a FoFNL initiative holding a Railway Conference in October 1995. Our representative had taken forward this initiative in the Partnership and the Steering Group.

At a recent Partnership meeting our Chairman, John Melling, offered the help of members to distribute flyer leaflets publicising the new service.

Newsletter June 1999

SERVICE PROVISION - SUMMER 1999 AND BEYOND

What has befallen the multi agency study of three years ago which identified level crossings and speed on entry to passing loops as areas for improvement? FoFNL looks to a Thurso - Inverness timing of 3 hours 30 minutes, even with the present traction equipment, and a Sunday evening train in each direction.

The recent Sunday trial with a 158 unit over the length of the line raises both opportunities and concerns. The capacity of these sets to run at 90 mph and accelerate more quickly from a stand offers potential time saving. Although the line is currently restricted to 75 mph the straighter layout in Easter Ross and between Georgemas and Wick should enable faster running. Together with faster acceleration away from stations can we expect a Thurso - Inverness timing of 3 hours 20 minutes, or even 3 hours 15 minutes, with commensurate reductions for Wick? The outcome of this trial conducted by the rail industry is awaited with interest.

John Melling

Newsletter February 2000

INTO THE MILLENNIUM

What has been achieved over the six short years since FoFNL was founded?

- freight the life blood of a rural railway, is back after eight silent years
- the Dingwall Commuter train, the first service to be introduced by ScotRail beyond its franchise agreement
- some improvements in journey time
- first steam train to Wick in over 30 years
- purposeful representation at RUCC (Rail Users' Consultative Committee) and other bodies
- initiation of, and membership of Highland Railway Partnership

FoFNL has taken a lead in each of these spheres, through lobbying, advocacy or action. The Far North Line is on the map!

The first year of the new millennium holds good prospects for:

- an open access Freight Terminal in Caithness
- a daily freight train including Safeway Refrigerated Boxes
- regular timber loading at Kinbrace
- 15 minutes off end to end passenger train journeys
- go ahead for the station at Beauly

Each of these developments represents investment by stakeholders, a sign of confidence in the future

33

of rail.

But FoFNL has further objectives including:

- extending the morning commuter train to start from Tain
- a station at Conon Bridge/Maryburgh
- an all year round end to end Sunday afternoon train in each direction
- improved frequencies in Easter Ross with bus connections for Dornoch
- signalling the eastern approach to Platform 5 at Inverness to improve through running
- easing of planning restrictions on rail access at Invergordon harbour

Some of these will require significant work with government, planners, and the railway industry. We are fortunate in that our founder, Frank Roach, is now the North Highland Railway Development Officer.

2000 AD opens with a series of meetings with Community Councils. An ear to the ground and local dialogue should be helpful to both FoFNL and local communities in working for a better railway. If you, too, have ideas please write to the the the Newsletter Editor or the Secretary.

John Melling

Newsletter September 2000

TAIN COMMUTER

Another FoFNL goal achieved - the Tain Commuter train starts on 25th September. With support from ScotRail FoFNL designed and produced the promotional leaflet. By mid September over 3000 copies had been distributed - 2100 to Invergordon homes as insertions in the Community Council Newsletter, and 1000 in Alness enclosed with the Community Association Newsletter. We wish ScotRail well in developing this service. This could be the beginning of improved services around the Moray Firth.

Photo: Andrew Allan

Also mentioned, in passing:

FoFNL welcomed the May 2000 timetable with its average reduction of 18 minutes in Wick-Inverness travel time and is pleased this is consolidated for 2000-2001.

Newsletter January 2001

ANOTHER TRIUMPH FOR YOUR COMMITTEE

Photo: Roger Piercy

After a period of local unsettlement the official announcement to re-open Beauly Station took place on 19th January at a press launch attended by the Rt. Hon. Charles Kennedy MP in whose constituency the station is situated.

Your committee convened meetings in Beauly and the Highland Council Chamber to further the cause of the re-opening. Beauly had missed out on funding several times in the past but funding of £84,000 from the Strategic Rail Authority along with Railtrack (£67,000), Highland Council (£30,000), Inverness and Nairn Enterprise (£18,000) and

Highland Rail Developments (£5,000) means that the project can now go ahead.

The station will consist of a 10m platform, a waiting shelter and small car park. It is expected that it will be used most regularly by travellers to Inverness for work and leisure with seven trains each way, six days a week providing the service.

ScotRail Press Release, Spring 2001

GOOD NEWS FOR SUNDAY WINTER TRAVELLERS

ScotRail is to run as a commercial venture throughout the 2001/2 winter a first-ever year-round Sunday train each way between Wick, Thurso and Inverness on a trial use-it-or-lose-it basis.

Likely timings would maximise journey opportunities for people taking the train in either direction to return from a weekend away. Connections would be available at Inverness from Glasgow, Edinburgh and Aberdeen to the North - and from the North to Glasgow, Edinburgh, Edinburgh and the Caledonian Sleeper service to London.

The new service will call at the usual intermediate stations plus the reopened Beauly Station.

ScotRail Managing Director, Alastair McPherson says "We are delighted to be able to respond from many requests by the Friends of the Far North Line and other community representatives by introducing at our own risk this winter Sunday service for the Far North."

Newsletter October 2001

PROMOTING THE FAR NORTH LINE

Your committee has been busy publicising two major events on the Far North Line. For the introduction of the winter Sunday service an A5 leaflet was produced and samples sent to all the Community Councils along the line asking for help in distributing the leaflets and publicity in the form of articles in their newsletters. All the local papers were contacted and a supply of leaflets were sent to Raigmore Hospital and the Colleges in Thurso and Inverness. Committee members distributed leaflets to shops and public places in Thurso, Wick, Golspie, Brora, Helmsdale, Tain, Invergordon and Alness. The northbound commuter train on consecutive Fridays was also leafleted.

For the re-opening of Beauly Station we will be distributing leaflets to all households with the co-operation of the Beauly Community Council. The delay in opening the station is due to increased costs incurred on the approach roadway to the station. At the latest Highland Rail Partnership meeting FoFNL was pushing for a speedy resolution to this problem.

EWS Press Release, Autumn 2001

EWS INVESTMENT

EWS (English Welsh & Scottish Railway, now part of DB Cargo UK), Britain's leading rail freight operator, is to invest £50,000 upgrading the Far North rail line from Thurso - Georgemas for operation of the new Class 66 rail freight locomotive.

Currently, the Class 66 locomotive is only cleared to operate as far as Georgemas. The extension to Thurso will open up new rail freight opportunities and remove many trucks from the Highland road network. The £50,000 investment by EWS will expand the route availability of its new locomotives. Work to upgrade the route will be completed in October.

Graham Smith, EWS Planning Director, said: "The clearance of this route shows the commitment of EWS to invest in order to secure rail freight growth. Key customers in Thurso have been identified by EWS and once infrastructure work has been completed, trucks will be removed from many main Highland roads including the A9 as a result of this investment."

66096 in Thurso, December 2002. Photo: Duncan Stewart

Newsletter May 2002

BEAULY

15th April 2002 saw three openings on one day - Beauly station, the Thurso freight yard and although at a distance, the Malcolm Group Rail Container depot at Grangemouth. The first two bring direct benefit to the line and the third potentially so. Scottish Ministers attended the latter two with Lewis Macdonald performing the rites at Thurso.

By contrast the opening of Beauly station was low key. FoFNL was represented by Roger Piercy, Newsletter Editor, one of whose photographs appears in this issue. Some years earlier after meeting the Beauly Community Council, Frank Roach, then Secretary of FoFNL had advocated a station; your committee pursued it; the Highland Railway Partnership became committed; and the rail industry, Enterprise bodies and Highland Council funded it. Today this simple station serves as a beacon of public service and environmental good.

FoFNL would like to thank all those who carried through intricate negotiations whether locally or nationally. There were difficulties from which learning can be drawn. Some thoughts are:-

1. transport planning includes environmental as well as socio-economic assessment

2. whilst project development includes customer specification, design work and planning approval, specific reactions from relevant quasi-governmental bodies are needed along the way

3. planning, design, construction and commissioning take longer than people recognise

4. however thorough consultation 'you can not please all the people all the time'

FoFNL hopes this small station will be an exemplar for future rural rail station development. For now may the people of Beauly enjoy using their station.

John Melling

Photo: Roger Piercy

[Beauly was the first station on the line to be reopened for quite a while and represented a major success for Frank Roach in achieving a temporary (now normalised) derogation for such a short platform.]

Newsletter May 2004

HEADCODE

With this issue of the newsletter you will find a photocopy of our first issue of ten years ago. It is interesting to see that many of the same matters are still being discussed but also that many have been implemented. A Highland Rail Partnership has been established; freight is back on the line; the Highland Railcard, services to Beauly, and the Tain commuter have all been very successful. We would claim that FoFNL advocacy has been a significant factor. However, Conon reopening and a Dornoch Link are still only possibilities for the future.

Richard Ardern

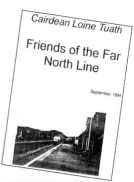

FoFNL would have been horrified to have known then that in 2019 the timings would still be extended - quickest: 4hr 10min, slowest: 4hr 31min.

FoFNL Press Release 15 May 2005

THE SLOW TRAIN

The Friends of the Far North Line today expressed surprise that First ScotRail (FSR) are to decelerate the trains from Wick to Inverness by so much as twenty to twenty five minutes end to end when the new timetable comes into force on 12 June. The original suggestion was that it would be less than ten minutes.

The slow down has been brought about by new safety procedures introduced over the last year. FoFNL concedes that safety is vitally important but considers that Network Rail should have introduced the "over-speed sensors" which have helped to alleviate a similar situation in Wales. So much extra time is being added here that three and three quarter hours from Thurso and four and one quarter hours from Wick to Inverness are not attractive journey times to encourage passengers.

The morning trains will leave from Wick at 06:23 and from Inverness at 07:14 which is too early for many passengers. Maybe FSR should now provide a sleeping car available from 22:00 for Wickers (They will already be providing a connection from Thurso to Wick at 21:30) so that passengers can get a good night's sleep and wake up well on their way to Inverness!

The new 10:39 gives a more useful departure time from Inverness than 11:27 but this now leaves a gap of over SEVEN HOURS until the next train which is not an acceptable level of service. This strongly reinforces FoFNL's case for reintroducing a fourth train leaving Wick at around 08:30 and returning from Inverness at 14:00 to provide civilised starting times and good boat connections.

The retimed 17:43 from Inverness will miss by five minutes an incoming service from the Aberdeen line making passengers catch the previous service and wait nearly 2½ hours. Again this underlines that the provision of an hourly interval service on the Aberdeen line is long overdue having first been promised in 1994.

FoFNL welcomes the new status of Alness and Fearn as mandatory stops and calls for a good bus connection to be provided from the Seaboard villages to Fearn to connect with the welcome new Invernet services to be introduced in December.

Together with the poor standard of rolling stock currently used, these timetable changes underline the need for major investment on the line. FoFNL would suggest that this could start with the construction of the Georgemas curve direct to Thurso and with the ordering of new rolling stock fit for the needs of the line. That includes much greater passenger comfort, increased luggage space and bicycle space which recognises the popularity of cycling in the area and the unique John O'Groats\Land's End cycling factor.

FoFNL believes Network Rail should also be required to improve the points and signalling so that the slow crawl into each loop can be speeded up. They should also examine intermediate speed limits to see

[Left] Beautiful as long as it doesn't get any worse!
Train leaving Muir of Ord on 9 December 2017.
Photo: Sandy Colley

[Below] The Beast From the East arrived on 28 February 2018.

Facing up to the snow

Forsinard, photo: Jonathan Ford

Photo: Michael 'Bubz' Mackay and Rob Kay

WINTER ON THE FAR NORTH LINE

Clearing the points at Brora

Route proving, Lairg

Photos: Network Rail

where quick win improvements to line speed could be made.

FoFNL considers that this slow new timetable should be seen as a short temporary measure and that strenuous efforts should be made by the rail companies to speed the trains up again. This serious situation reinforces the case for an Executive sponsored overall survey of how infrastructure and services on the line could best be improved to adequately serve the various markets of local people, tourists and travellers to Orkney. In conclusion, FoFNL has suggested to First ScotRail that they should offer some compensation to their regular loyal customers for this major inconvenience.

Newsletter September 2005

SPEEDING UP AGAIN

When the June deceleration was explained at the Rail Passengers Committee's public meeting in Dingwall in May, we were told that the Scottish Transport Minister had instructed Network Rail to seek to restore the previous line speed in early course. Since then, the Office of Rail Regulation wrote to Network Rail (NR) on 8 July setting out that company's obligations. In particular: "Network Rail must maintain routes to the published capability level at April 2001" and "If operators want to run more trains of the same type on a route, NR is responsible for any increase in maintenance needed. NR must not charge operators extra for this". To my mind, the "published capability level" would include, not just the number of trains, but the end to end timings. Let us hope that ScotRail will request a return to the "capability" of Wick to Inverness journeys taking less than four hours.

Richard Ardern

[Unfortunately the promised "speeding up" didn't happen and fourteen years later we're still waiting!]

Newsletter January 2006

HEADCODE - NEW CONVENER'S INTRODUCTION

2005 was a difficult year for the Friends of the Far North Line. A great deal of the Committee's time was occupied with internal matters which became so heated that the Chairman was forced to resign through ill health. I am glad to say that Richard Ardern is now restored to full operational capacity and that he has been re-elected to the Committee. His experience will be essential to restoring FoFNL to full operational capacity as well.

When I moved to Thurso in November 2005 I was blissfully unaware that the Friends were about to elect me as your Chairman. When I began to understand the unhappy state of affairs, however, I decided that my experience of dealing with the whole range of passenger aspirations ought to be made available to my local bit of the railway. Having been booted out of office by the government, along with about 150 others across Great Britain, my first inclination was to mutter darkly about never bothering to do public things again, but the black mood soon passed and here I am writing this Introduction. I am happy to say that I served only about 60 seconds as your Chairman before the AGM agreed with my request that the office be called that of Convener henceforth. And no nonsense about the Constitution not saying so!

So what am I planning to do? First and foremost to heal the wounds. FoFNL is a broad church capable of holding people with differing views and viewpoints. What I will not tolerate as Convener, however, is disruption of the aims and objectives of the Friends. We are all subservient to those.

The other immediate objective, which will have taken place by the time you read these words, is to make once and for all a clear and unambiguous statement about FoFNL's position on the building of a Dornoch Link. It is this:

FoFNL believes that the Scottish Executive should issue tenders for a full appraisal of the costs and benefits, including socio-economic benefits, of improvements to the service on the Far North Line. This should include, but not be confined to, the building of a Dornoch Link. FoFNL will support any reasonable moves from other bodies and parties which seek to persuade the Scottish Executive to adopt this policy.

Having let everyone know that this is our policy we can then leave the Dornoch Link to one side for the couple of years or so before a thorough appraisal would be published. This will free the Committee - and members - to concentrate on the myriad small things which can be done to improve the line, and the service offered along it. Highland Rail Partnership has been instrumental in delivering the new Invernet service at the southern end (if Lairg can be so called) of the Line. The FoFNL Committee was successful in its request for a fourth train south from Caithness. We should build on this and seek the next phase of improvements on the route.

I intend to meet senior figures at Network Rail, First ScotRail and Her Majesty's Railway Inspectorate to discover exactly what and where the obstacles to a faster service are. Some are geographical and buried in the lairdly folklore of a bygone age. Others, however, are depressingly recent and in my mind eminently capable of yielding to rational examination. Lord Cullen's requirements leading to a thoughtless blanket application of TPWS is a case in point.

This is a rather longer Introduction than is usual, or than I intend it to be in future. However, I think it's important at this stage in the Friends' history to set out where I intend to lead members over the next year or two. I hope to have your support and I look forward to meeting as many of you as possible at our various meetings and outings in 2006.

Mike Lunan

Newsletter September 2006

FoFNL Response to Room For Growth Study

[Extract] In essence FoFNL accepts that in the absence of a pot of external (to the rail industry) money the £73m +/- 50% (excluding signalling) needed to build the Dornoch link is so far away from an acceptable CBA figure as to make it hard to justify further expenditure unless it can be shown that Room for Growth has somehow failed to take all relevant factors into account. FoFNL does not take this view, although it is aware that others may do. Nonetheless the Dornoch link is bound to remain a long-term objective of Caithness-based economic forums of one sort or another.

FoFNL is much keener to involve itself, and expend energy, in lending support to the many smaller schemes for speeding up trains on the FNL outlined in the documents - speeding up loop entry/exit and eliminating many of the unnecessary speed restrictions at level crossings. We believe that modest, but nonetheless useful, savings can be achieved at relatively small cost.

Mike Lunan

The following item from 2006 is a typical example of the work FoFNL does, responding to various reports and proposals. We have a web page [http://www.fofnl.org.uk/archives/respsub.php] with links to several of these from past years but reprinting this one in full gives a good idea of the depth of involvement FoFNL maintains.

Regional Transport Strategy: Highlands & Islands

Friends of the Far North Line (FoFNL) is pleased to have this opportunity to comment on HITRANS's draft Regional Transport Strategy (RTS). FoFNL, formed in 1994 to support the railway line from Inverness to Thurso and Wick, has a membership strength of 200, including several community councils. It has recently successfully lobbied for the new fourth daily train service south from Wick and for substantive refurbishment of the train sets currently used on the line.

FoFNL believes that significant infrastructure investment is required on the Far North Line (FNL) both in track improvements and in signalling. It is profoundly disappointing that the end to end journey time had to be extended by some 25 minutes nearly two years ago due partly to new speed restrictions through the passing loops. It is vitally important that this set back is reversed, as the railway needs to be speeded up to compete with a road made quicker due to continuing substantial investment projects such as the Dornoch road bridge.

Scott Wilson's Room For Growth study (R4G) published by HIE in June 2006 advances several major improvements which would be justified to speed up the line and increase capacity to ensure greater robustness to the timetable. These are:

- Reinstated loop or double track through Lentran
- Raising line speed throughout
- Upgraded loop speeds
- Upgraded level crossings
- Constructing a direct chord to the Thurso line at Georgemas Junction

FoFNL considers that all these works are necessary together with

Upgrading the signalling system (including a replacement for the RETB system).

The radio signalling system known as Radio Electronic Token Block was installed in 1984 at a time when traffic was much lighter. Its current state is now a major impediment to further development of a line which has seen a 30% increase in passenger numbers in the past three years and more passenger trains being run. Technology has moved on so much in twenty years, and the system only has the one console such that only one train movement can be dealt with at a time. Trains are often delayed waiting to obtain clearance to proceed. This is clearly most unsatisfactory.

The Scott Wilson report considered that there is a very good case for reinstating the loop or double track through Lentran, but did not advance it to final recommendation stage because of worries that the RETB system would simply collapse if anything further were added! FoFNL considers it to be unacceptable that the line should be handicapped in such a way.

FoFNL therefore requests that the two schemes to

- Replace RETB and upgrade the signalling system
- Reinstate the loop or double track through Lentran

should please be included in the HITRANS Regional Transport Strategy for feasibility and design work to commence during the 2007/12 period with delivery during that period also if at all possible. This is urgent work for the Far North Line.

FoFNL would suggest that consideration be given to extending the Inverness colour light signalling from Clachnaharry through to Dingwall where the Far North and Kyle lines diverge. Thereafter, a replacement radio signalling system with spare capacity for the future might be used. It should be noted that these projects would benefit both the Far North and the Kyle lines. The increase in capacity and the considerable reduction in the number of delays caused to passengers by the 13 mile and 20 minute long single section from Inverness to Muir of Ord are both desperately needed now. The 10 mph limit over the Clachnaharry swing bridge contributes to the slow journey time over this pivotal section for both Far North and Kyle lines.

FoFNL welcomes the inclusion of a reopened station at Conon Bridge in the HITRANS RTS proposals. FoFNL pays tribute to HITRANS and its predecessor, the Highland Rail Partnership, for the funding they have put in to railway schemes such as platform shelters and bicycle stands over the past few years, and welcomes HITRANS's interest in funding the new stations at Dalcross and Conon Bridge. FoFNL also supports a Kyle arrival into Inverness just before 09.00.

FoFNL considers that it is seriously insufficient for a draft regional strategy for the next 17 years to be currently supporting only one station reopening and one retiming but no other work on a

41

fast expanding but seriously constricted line such as the FNL. We call upon HITRANS to include the signalling and continuing infrastructure developments outlined above in its RTS and would hope to see all of these completed long before the end of the seventeen year span of the RTS.

The urgently increasing importance of making greater use of public transport for passengers and rail transport for freight is accepted by all who think seriously about the future. The problems of scarcity of oil and the effects of climate change will be only too apparent by 2023, the end of the plan period. FoFNL considers that rail transport should have made a step change in increased use by then. One major limiting factor in the Highlands is the prevalence of single track rail lines. Just as this same problem was attacked in the last century by the Crofter Counties Roads Scheme, there is an urgent need to put in more lengths of double track and passing loops along the Highland rail routes which converge on the fast growing city region of Inverness.

Looking further to the future on the FNL, the one big project which would make a major difference for all users north of Rogart would be the Dornoch Link first proposed in the nineteen eighties. Although it does not score well in current project assessments, the much greater indispensability expected of rail in the future would be in its favour. A new organisation, independent of FoFNL, named the Dornoch Link Action Group, has recently been formed to pursue this. Future reopening of stations at Evanton, Dornoch and Halkirk would promote greater social inclusion, and reopening of loops at points such as Fearn, Kildonan and Altnabreac amongst others would enable much greater traffic flows of freight and passenger trains to be handled via Lairg and Dornoch.

FoFNL views the railways in the northern and eastern Highlands as one interlinked system pivoted on Inverness. It is important to the FNL that the railways to Aberdeen, and Perth and beyond are supported and improved. FoFNL welcomes the proposals in the RTS to speed up services and increase the frequencies to hourly on both these lines. Such hourly frequencies will make it much easier for passengers to connect to and from the FNL with its services to Wick, Kyle and the Easter Ross terminators. Speeding up does not necessarily mean diverting services under the runway at Edinburgh Airport. A halt on the existing line at Gogar would do. It is necessary to provide intercity standard of rolling stock on this line, equivalent in comfort to new versions of HST or Mark 3 stock.

The prospect of a new station at Inverness Airport is also welcomed by FoFNL as are the proposed extra services to and from Elgin. FoFNL considers that the long section from Nairn to Inverness should be provided with a loop at Dalcross or have the double track replaced onwards to Inverness. In addition to helping with potential timber traffic to the Morayhill factory, the loop/double track performs exactly the same performance improvements as would be the case at Lentran.

Single track imposes serious delay problems on trains when out of course running occurs. These delays can continue to affect running for the rest of the day as all trains are timed according to the timings of other trains for crossing purposes. Both the FNL and the Aberdeen lines have departures from Inverness timed for two minutes after an incoming service has arrived. The essential necessity of double track at both ends as exists on the Highland Main Line from Perth to Stanley and Culloden Moor to Inverness allows the timetable to be operated much more smoothly without delays to passengers. **Thus Lentran and Dalcross loops or double track are essential improvements for these other two Highland lines.**

FoFNL is delighted to see a number of major rail schemes advancing in the south of Scotland in recent years. Many commentators have noticed that the economic and social development benefits of similar schemes have not yet been made available to the Highlands. FoFNL believes HITRANS has done a good job with its own strategy for improvements on the Perth and Aberdeen lines. **The HITRANS RTS makes a good case for socio-economic benefits to be felt as far north as Inverness. In FoFNL's opinion HITRANS also needs to strengthen the case for similar benefits to be provided to passengers and freight operators on the Far North Line by supporting the early completion of the signalling and track improvements marked by bullet points above.**

© FoFNL 28 December 2006.

CARING FOR STATIONS

FoFNL is not the only organisation that cares for the line. Brora & District Action Group (BaDAG) field a working squad, seen here in August 2016, to improve the station platform environment.

The unique Dunrobin Castle Station has much care lavished on it!

Photo: Daniel Brittain-Catlin

Evidence of the work done by Alness Community Association in 2006 to make the station a much nicer place at which to wait or arrive.

Ardgay Station (*Bonar Bridge* until 2nd May 1977) on 1st October 2014 when ladies of the Kyle of Sutherland Heritage Society were at the station in period dress to celebrate the 150th anniversary of the opening of the station.

Photo: Sandy Colley

Useful description of what FoFNL does...at the halfway point from formation to now...

Newsletter September 2007

CONVENER'S AGM REPORT - 2007

Since we last met in Brora eight months ago the Committee has - yet again - found itself with a substantial work load. Three Newsletters have been produced which reported in outline what we've been up to.

The Network Rail Route Utilisation Strategy - the infrastructure blueprint for all the things which Network Rail think worth doing if the money is provided - was published shortly after last year's AGM. It was gratifying to see that some at least of the points FoFNL made in its response to the Consultation were taken on board. It remains to be seen how much priority the Secretary of State and the Scottish Government Ministers give to the list of schemes - we expect a major announcement within the next 10 days. Two, in fact, a High Level Output Statement (government-speak for shopping list) and a Statement of Funds Available (how much they have in their wallet). The fear is that the first will be all-encompassing but the second - with much wringing of hands - will say not yet. FoFNL will be making a public response in due course. There is so much that could be done for relatively little on the FNL, and we continue to press for a start to be made.

We responded in considerable detail to HITRANS's Regional Transport Strategy - another blueprint document. In simple terms, if a scheme isn't in the RTS it won't get funded. Again we were partially successful in ensuring that Inverness's eye was not wholly diverted away from Caithness and the Far North Line.

We published an extra Newsletter in April to coincide with the May Election campaigns. In it I spelt out a 30-year vision for all of Scotland's railway. It was sent to a much wider range of people than our normal Newsletters - indeed it went to all constituency candidates for the four largest parties and the top three in the regional lists. It was also sent to a selection of candidates for the Highland Council. How successful this extra effort will be won't be apparent for some time. Acorns have this dilatory habit. But it's a document we can point to in future and against which we can measure improvement. It will be interesting to see whether an extra Newsletter in 2011 will be full of praise or of disappointment.

As well as all this writing and policy-making I've continued to have meetings with the industry. Richard Ardern and I met Michelle Crawford, the new regional manager at Inverness. Later the same day we were among the audience at a passenger (or customer, as it's quaintly called) forum in Inverness chaired by James King of Passenger Focus. I've attended meetings, including the AGM, of Highland Rail Partnership and taken the opportunity that these meetings provide of networking (we used to call it hobnobbing) with various industry stakeholders (we used to call them colleagues). As you will have seen in the Newsletter I've been re-appointed to an industry safety body which meets three times a year in London - the grandly-named Rail Industry Advisory Committee. I used to serve on this until 2005 as a member of the old Rail Passengers Council, and it was gratifying to find that they apparently couldn't do without me. Much of the business is concerned with inward-facing matters like how guidance for industry workers should be written, but some of it is outward-facing, dealing with big safety issues like level crossing abuse. As we all know this is - sadly - a big problem on the FNL. We have over 80% of the most unprotected public road crossings in Scotland on the FNL and Kyle lines, and there's a huge education job still to be done in two areas. First, teaching road users that the train will always win in any collision with a car; and secondly, reminding the roads authority that they have a responsibility too. Fortunately the 2006 Act gives the Secretary of State power to require the roads authority to contribute towards level crossing upgrades. How he uses this power (or how Scottish Government Ministers use it) is something we're watching.

But the big effort in the last 8 months has been one in which many of you were involved as well. Some of you may have seen, or even travelled in, the first of the refurbished Class 158s. It appeared in Thurso earlier this month and my timing in getting pictures of it to the *John o'Groat Journal* on what was a quiet news day in Caithness ensured splash coverage on page 1. I am on record as giving it "8 out of 10". Nothing ever gets 10 in my book, and 9 was withheld because of the fact that the toilets continue to discharge onto the track. FoFNL mounted a vigorous public campaign earlier in the year to draw attention to this - a fact which clearly astonished many people - and many of you wrote to the papers and to politicians demanding an end to this outdated and disgusting practice. I'm glad to say as a result of this campaign, that there is a chink of light. We were told at the public meeting in Inverness that Network Rail - whose responsibility it is to clean the tracks, and whose employees get sprayed with the stuff - is prepared to fund half of the cost of the necessary work. It isn't a done deal yet, but I can't think it's very likely that First ScotRail would make such an announcement in public unless they were pretty convinced that something would be done fairly soon.

So I can report progress, albeit slow, on many fronts since last November. Some done; much still to do. I'd like to thank my Committee colleagues for all their work - Roger Piercy for his unfailingly excellent and informative Newsletters, Iain MacDonald for his insight into signalling and other technical track-related matters, Gavin Sinclair for his operational and timetabling input - often wholly unseen but nonetheless vital in informing our inputs into the Great December 2008 Revision (of which more next year), Angus and Janice Stewart for their formidable husband-and-wife team in keeping the membership records and making sure the money flows in, Anne Sutherland for her commuter experience (and legal expertise) and, last but certainly not least, Richard Ardern for his huge input to just about everything we do on your behalf, and on behalf of all rail passengers in these parts. Thank you to them and to all of you for your support.

Mike Lunan

The following two articles reflect a recurring theme of our campaigning. At the time of writing this publication we are highly optimistic that the building of a loop on that section of route is about to be confirmed...

Newsletter January 2007

LENTRAN LOOP: LYNCHPIN OF THE LINE?

FoFNL's immediate priorities are to build cases for the early replacement of the radio signalling system and for the capacity increase and greater operating efficiency which would stem from a double track crossing facility in the Lentran area. Last summer's Scott Wilson report made a very good case for this loop at an estimated cost of around £1m for a 200 metre long loop or £9m to redouble the whole six miles from Clachnaharry to Clunes. The additional signalling costs for each project would be a further £6m making totals of £7m or £15m for the two options. The only reason it was not amongst the final recommendations was due to fears that the 1985 RETB signalling system is so obsolete it might collapse if alterations were attempted.

FoFNL finds this quite unacceptable and has been lobbying for both the RETB replacement and the Lentran enhancement to be included in the Network Rail and HITRANS strategies. One attractive solution might be to extend the existing Inverness colour light signals from Clachnaharry to Clunes, Muir or even Dingwall.

The present 13 mile single track section from Inverness to Muir takes 20 minutes partly because of the very slow speed limit over the Caledonian Canal swing bridge. Some of the margins at Inverness between an incoming arrival and an outgoing departure are as little as two minutes. There is no room for late running. A delay to the morning 06.22 from Wick due at 10.37 can delay the 10.39 to Wick. This can consequently delay the 08.13 from Wick at Invergordon and it has a crucial crossing with the 12.37 from Wick at Forsinard where there is a 35 minute single line section to Helmsdale. If the 12.37, due in to Inverness at 16.49 is late, it can delay the 16.55 connection to Glasgow. Indeed, the whole process could equally have started with the 07.07 from Glasgow due Inverness at 10.26 being more than 12 minutes late arriving. A delay in Glasgow in the morning can be reflected back to Glasgow that same evening.

This is why the restoration of a double track section through Lentran is of such vital importance. Creating extra capacity for freight in particular and avoidance of inconvenience and extra cost to both passengers and the railway in making alternative arrangements when trains are late underlines the need for the enhancement.

Richard Ardern

Newsletter September 2007

The Lentran Loop

Explanation of why it's so important from Iain MacDonald, FoFNL Committee Member and retired signalman.

One of the items on FoFNL's wish list is the provision of a loop at Lentran. I thought some observations about an additional loop to ease train operations between Inverness and Dingwall would be of interest to our readers.

Prior to RETB signalling a loop was provided at Lentran when the line was converted to single track from Clunes to Clachnaharry. This was an excellent location for a crossing point for trains between Inverness and Muir of Ord and its main drawback was that it was too short for long freight trains coming off the North at night (changed days!). Another problem was that on the UP leg of the loop was a set of sprung trap points, which made any shunting movements rather awkward. Why the loop needed to be so short I don't know, as the trackbed existed, it having been a double line, so it was only a case of selecting the length of track and putting points at each end. The most likely reason was that it was required to operate the loop from a single points cabin using manual rodding to change the points which limits the distance from lever to points, otherwise a motor would be needed at one end or two cabins operated by one man. A rather antiquated system which most loops north of Dingwall used.

The benefit today for installing this loop with its hydraulic sprung points (HSC) would be to cross trains halfway between Muir of Ord loop and Inverness Station, enabling trains to be dispatched north without having to either wait for a late running southbound train to arrive or to further delay the southbound train at Muir of Ord when dispatching the northbound train on time which exacerbates the problem of missing connections east and south.

Lentran is almost half way between Inverness and Muir of Ord and for simplicity in the following example I will assume the journey time is 10 minutes Inverness to Lentran and 11 minutes Lentran to Muir of Ord. There are many scenarios that will develop with late running trains between Inverness and Muir of Ord but we will take the example of Train A waiting at Muir of Ord to travel to Inverness and at the same time Train B is ready to be despatched from Inverness to Muir of Ord. Under the current situation one of those trains will incur a delay of 21 minutes whilst waiting for the other to traverse the section. If it is the northbound train that is delayed we now incur problems the whole length of the line as it will be out of place at the planned crossing points and if it is the southbound train there is an increased risk of passengers missing connections and there is every chance that it will be the southbound train that is running late and causing all the problems. But, with the Lentran Loop both trains can be despatched towards Lentran at the same time with the northbound train arriving first and waiting 1 minute for the southbound to cross thereby saving the further loss of 21 minutes.

This is for crossing purposes only, nothing would be gained for trains following each other as Clunes is a token exchange point and as soon as a train passes clear of the prescribed point the section is then clear for the next train to follow. The next thing is we would lose some time by having to go over the HSC at the mandatory reduced speed. Is it value for money? Possibly not. But it is an essential part of the infrastructure and has only been denied to keep the cost down of the original RETB scheme. I'm sure your committee will make strenuous efforts to have this anomaly rectified.

Iain MacDonald

WE AWAIT THE TIME

Iain Coucher, Mike Lunan, Nigel Harris (Editor: *RAIL*) and John Thurso. Photo: Roger Piercy

"We must find and exploit real opportunities to reduce journey times." - **Iain Coucher**, Chief Executive of Network Rail, speaking in a Far North Line context at the FoFNL AGM in Inverness, 30 June 2008.

Newsletter September 2008

CONVENER'S AGM REPORT

We have been in detailed talks with First ScotRail about the timetable, not least the long-awaited provision of a 4th train north from Inverness to Caithness. This will start in December, leaving Inverness shortly before 2 o'clock, bridging the 7-hour gap between existing departures. It will be possible to have breakfast - admittedly an early one - in Caithness, spend an hour and a half in Inverness - long enough for many tasks - and get home in time for tea. It will also allow Orkney folk to get the late ferry home from Scrabster. I don't think this train, or the 4th train south introduced a couple of years ago, would be in the timetable without FoFNL's pressure.

Mike Lunan

Newsletter January 2009

2008 SURVEY OF FAR NORTH LINE DELAYS

One of the characteristics of the Far North Line is that when a delay occurs it can affect the service for the rest of the day. This is because the line is single track and there are variable, sometimes very long, distances between passing loops.

The FoFNL Committee has been concerned for some time about the number of train failures and signalling faults that have been affecting the performance of services on the line. Throughout 2008 we have been recording all the incidents of which we became aware. We have now done an initial assessment of performance during the 49 weeks of the last timetable from 1 January until 13 December 2008.

It must be clearly understood that the results are only a pointer to what has been happening. They give some idea that the scale of the problem might be anything upwards from say 1.5 times as much as this. We do not have full data to know how many train delays there were, nor do we know the total delay minutes caused and how these are apportioned. We recorded 190 delays:

Train faults	65
Signalling faults	32
Points/track faults	7
TOTAL RESOURCE FAILINGS	104

47

Staff shortages	11
TOTAL DIRECT FAILINGS	115
Consequential delays	52
TOTAL OPERATOR FAILINGS	167
Unknown or outwith railway control e.g. obstructions	23
TOTAL SERVICES AFFECTED	190
Percentages:	%
Train faults	34.2
Network Rail faults	20.5
Staff shortages	5.8
Consequential delays	27.5

This gives a frequency of recorded delays (unknown fraction of actual) of 4 per week. Removing the consequential delays reveals an average of 3 direct causal incidents per week.

We know that the Invernet services are often sacrificed when FSR is short of a unit at Inverness. Eleven Invernet services were cancelled throughout as were 13 ex-Wick services (most frequently the 08.13 WCK-INV). In addition to this there were a further 11 occasions when the train did not call at Thurso due to late running. [The figure for the 12 months to the date of compiling *FoFNL 25* was **53**!]

We already knew that passengers suffer delays (sometimes long delays) and missed connections several times most weeks. We knew anecdotally that passengers' confidence in the service is diminished by this and that this includes the regular users such as the commuters who probably contribute the most as individuals to the line's revenue.

Having got some measure of the problems over a whole year, the Committee is to contact FSR and Network Rail to ask if some improvements can be made. Although the 158 fleet is ageing rapidly, and the faults are many and varied (ranging from a defective horn to flat batteries or a loss of coolant), we think it likely that performance can be improved even if it means stationing a fitter at Wick or having them travel on the trains. Whether NR can improve the performance of the RETB system is more difficult to assess. It is obsolete and long overdue for replacement.

The survey has shown to our satisfaction that it is high time to start planning the future investment for the next decade. A replacement for RETB is urgent. Increased line capacity can best be gained by reducing the distances between loops. This is already critical between Inverness and Dingwall and we are calling for the reinstatement of some of the former double track between Clachnaharry and Clunes including the former Lentran loop. The 158s cannot go on for ever so it is also time to start designing a new train especially for the longer rural tourist lines and in time for the next franchise. We trust that Transport Scotland will engage with us over these urgent imperatives.

Working in FoFNL sometimes gives members opportunities to see, and understand, what goes into running a railway. Bob Barnes-Watts, Mike Lunan and Richard Ardern were welcomed on board the Network Rail Track Recording Unit in January 2009.

Newsletter May 2009

TESTING THE TRACK TO WICK

It was a sunny January morning when I met Mike Lunan and Richard Ardern at Inverness station for a trip on the Far North Line to Wick. This time we would not be travelling on the 1038 ScotRail service, but on a Network Rail Track Recording Unit.

Unit 950001 was berthed in platform 7, resplendent in a yellow livery and with the sound of the generator, used to power the many electronic devices associated with maintaining a comprehensive record of the condition of the track, adding to the more recognisable 'engine noise'.

Thanks to an invitation from Ian Barber of Network Rail, we were privileged to be able to get a 'driver's eye view' of the line. Ian was unable to join us on the day but we were welcomed on board by Eddy Locke who gave us a thorough briefing on how everything worked on board this unit, a purpose-built train based on the Class 150 'Sprinter' design.

Apart from the 'technical gubbins' on board, the train has a large kitchen, vital for the crew who spend a lot of time on the train as it visits many rail lines on a 6 monthly basis. While we were sipping coffee and the unit was travelling alongside the Beauly Firth, Eddy was explaining that, apart from the electronic methods of recording the track condition, there was also a small compartment containing an electro pneumatic pump and water based paint mixture! This is still used as a method of visually identifying to the local track Engineers the location of particularly 'rough' stretches of track, whereby paint is fired onto the track in the four foot within 22 yards of an actionable defect,

which is still in use in 2009, however the teams are also advised of these location using modern high tech Global Positioning System co-ordinates as well as miles and chains.

Just as my head was reeling with the amount of technical information I was hoping to assimilate, we were invited to the front cab from where we could see just how much concentration is required to drive a train. The Far North Line has various sections of differing speeds, both permanent and temporary, and excellent route knowledge is needed to make sure all those

restrictions are observed.

Mike and I spent some time in the rear cab simply looking at where we had been and getting a different perspective of the Flow Country.

The train ran to time throughout and we alighted at Wick around 1530. Unfortunately we were unable to get a cab view of the line between Georgemas and Thurso due to time constraints but, hopefully, we may be invited on a future trip.

I'm pleased to say that, from what I could see of the recording instruments, the Far North Line is in pretty good nick! Further engineering work will be taking place this year to relay more sections of the line with continuous welded rail, making journeys even more smooth.

Our thanks to both Ian and Eddy and the on-train engineers and other crew who made us so welcome.

Article and photos by Bob Barnes-Watts

Mike Lunan's first 'swansong' *Headcode*!

Newsletter May 2009

HEADCODE

This is my thirteenth - and last - Headcode: I shall be handing over the Convenership to new hands in July. It seems a good time to review what FoFNL has achieved in the 3½ years since I was elected in November 2005, and to offer an idea of what the Promised Land might look like.

FoFNL itself was in some turmoil - the vexed question of the Dornoch Link divided the members. The 2005 AGM polarized the position, with around 40% of those present clearly in favour. When their candidate was defeated many left FoFNL, but the loss in members was much lower than 40% - clearly the activists had few supporters among the membership as a whole. A new body was formed by these activists, with its primary purpose being the promotion of the Dornoch Link. I have always taken the view that, however attractive on paper such an idea might be, in the real world of limited funds and competing priorities it is a non-starter. The impact of the recession merely strengthens my conviction. We have seen that CP4 (railway-speak for the period 2009-14) will have no spare money for anything big - the new Forth Crossing will see to that. The clever trick will be to ensure that good ideas are worked up during the early stages of planning for CP5 (2014-19), which as far as I am concerned starts now. FoFNL's agenda must be the identification, and promotion, of projects which have a chance of ticking the boxes within Network Rail and First ScotRail. FoFNL is now a body with its eyes focused on the achievable.

As far as the railway is concerned FoFNL can point to some significant improvements. Not all of these, of course, have been achieved by FoFNL on its own. Part of the skill of your Committee is its ability to work with other industry partners and funders, adding our weight to doors which are already creaking open. Among these have been the substantial input to the specification for the mid-life refurbishment of the Inverness-based 158s. These now have doubled cycle space and improved toilets and interior fittings. The main change, however, which was certainly FoFNL's, was to ensure that seats were aligned with windows (which brought the additional benefit of making them slightly further apart). Most passengers probably don't notice this - after all, it's how trains always used to be - but sitting in a Voyager gazing at a window deadlight is no fun. It's worth noting that the Haymarket-based 158 refurbs do not have this improved layout. We were successful in persuading Transport Scotland that our long straggly touristy line was worth spending a bit more money on.

There are now four trains a day in each direction. No longer does the Caithnessian who has an hour's business in Inverness have to twiddle his thumbs for six wasted hours before returning home. The extra morning train south means an extra welcome 90 minutes in bed before setting out. The extra trains connect with the Orkney ferry at Scrabster, so the benefits are felt in Orkney as well as along the FNL itself.

The unseen, but not unsmelt, benefit for which FoFNL can claim all the plaudits is the installation of retention-tank toilets on our 158s. The story has been told in previous Newsletters, and doesn't need to be repeated here, but it stands as a good instance of allowing a bit of unfocused outrage to be translated, by involving the Press and by getting people to write letters to politicians, into simple straightforward action. That it cost a couple of million quid means that FoFNL's gratitude (and that of all passengers, lineside workers and residents) is all the greater.

But it's not all joy: there's still a lot to be done. In the short term (CP4, say) there are myriad small schemes (a few tens of thousands of pounds) which would speed things up - a minute here, a minute there. FoFNL reckons that 25 minutes could be shaved off a ludicrously long journey time without spending serious money (serious is when you get to several million). In the medium term (CP5) there is a crying need for a bit of serious spending in building in robustness to the approach to Inverness (railway-speak for eliminating delays to services caused by a delay somewhere else). Redoubling the line from the swing bridge at Clachnaharry out to Clunes would be a huge step forward, but even a loop at Lentran would deliver significant improvement (and, in the long term, save money). In the long term we have to notice that a "mid-life" rolling stock refurb takes us only to about 2022 or so. We need a new train by then. But the Inverness allocation (which is by no means confined to the FNL and Kyle Line) is only 24 sets - far too small a production run. FoFNL has begun to address this need, and has thought about other similar lines whose rolling stock needs are similar - seasonal tourist traffic with luggage, cycles and an inexplicable desire to look out of the window, eat and so forth. There is a lot of rolling stock trundling around the branch lines of the network whose clapped-out-ness is much greater than that of our 158s, and a coalition of needs will be a good one to establish.

The railway, perilous though the nation's finances be, is in good heart. In Scotland, thanks to 10 years of forward-looking government, it has seen substantial growth both in size and business. The political will to go on improving isn't likely to disappear whatever may happen south of the Border. High-speed rail between Scotland and London is on the agenda of all parties, although one shouldn't prepare the sandwiches for the first run just yet. Closer to home the need is to remind politicians that a railway running through only three parliamentary constituencies is just as important as one running through dozens, even though it may carry fewer passengers. I am confident that your next Convener and the Committee will be up to the task, and I wish them well. I've had enormous fun - may they do so too.

Mike Lunan

It's always useful to look back - it gives encouragement for the future!
The rest of this comprehensive article can be read at www.fofnl.org.uk/newsletters/10May/10may08.php

FNE May 2010

A Future for Highland Lines

The past 15 years since the FoFNL conference has seen a renaissance in the fortunes of the railways north of Perth. The persistence of environmentally aware campaigners, such as FoFNL founder member Frank Spaven, has paid off. The FoFNL conference led to the establishment of the Rail Development Officer post filled by Frank Roach and then to the Highland Rail Partnership.

We have seen the highly successful reopening of Beauly station, now with 52,000 passenger journeys per year. Invernet was a ground breaking project won by Frank Roach, providing an all day service of local trains through Dingwall as far as Ardgay and Lairg. There are now three commuter trains arriving in Inverness from the north before 9am in the mornings. Given the Kessock Bridge queues on the A9 and parking congestion in Inverness, this is a very good thing.

FoFNL was established in 1994 and can claim numerous lobbying successes such as originating the idea of a fourth train each way to Wick connecting with new Northlink ferry schedules to Orkney; suggesting how the interiors of class 158s should be redesigned to give much greater passenger comfort and more bike space for end to enders; and very publicly campaigning for the fitting of retention toilets. [It is amazing what you can achieve if you kick up a stink!] We are now campaigning for the reinstatement of a passing loop from Lentran-Clunes in the middle of the long constraining single track section immediately north of Inverness. This would allow more trains to be run and greatly reduce delays at times of late running. FoFNL sees the Highland Lines north and east from Perth and Aberdeen as an inter-dependent network and keeps a watching brief there also. There are no other rail user groups covering the full length of those two lines.

The *Room for Growth* report completed in 2006 by Scott Wilson Railways for HIE has been an influential milestone. Two projects, the Highland Main Line (HML) upgrade scheduled for completion by **December 2011**, and rail service enhancements between Aberdeen and Inverness by **2016** are priorities in the Government's Strategic Transport Projects Review published in December 2008.

Richard Ardern

50049 (masquerading as long scrapped 50012 Benbow) winds round the reverse curves at Kinbrace heading the Inverness to Wick *Orcadian* on 18 June 2006.

Photo: Martin Loader

Class 52 D1015 *Western Champion* near Clachnaharry with the *Western Chieftain* tour on 20 June 2009.

Photo: Sandy Colley

Deltic 55022 *Royal Scots Grey* dressed as 55003 *Meld*, approaching Dingwall with the *Royal Scotsman* on 28 April 2015.

Photo: Sandy Colley

HEADCODE

As we enter a new year, it would be nice to think that progress is being made towards the enhanced services on both the Highland main line and on the Aberdeen line but, as you can see from Richard Ardern [in the next extract], we seem to be further away than ever, despite promises to the contrary from the politicians. In fact, rail seems to have disappeared almost entirely from the SNP government's agenda. At best, it's indifferent and, at worst, it's hostile. Our brief, of course, is the Far North Line but we cannot ignore the other routes into Inverness as, without them, we would be isolated. In the coming year, committee members will continue to lobby through the media to ensure that we keep a high profile and remind those who make the decisions that we are still here.

The committee has continued to work on its proposals for an hourly train service between Inverness and Tain. We feel that we have probably gone as far as we can with the existing infrastructure. The timetable that we have produced has a few elements in it that are less than ideal but we feel that we have done the best we can so far. Our next stage will be to see how we can address these by proposing infrastructure enhancements. These do not have to be expensive but would be geared towards saving minutes and half-minutes here and there. There is a parallel to this. When the Deltics first started work on the East Coast Main Line in 1961, the target time between London and Edinburgh was six hours with a one-stop, 11-coach train. By the time they were replaced by HSTs in the late 1970s, this journey time had come down to five hours, twenty-three minutes. In fact, it was a little better than that because, by then, the locomotives were supplying electric train heating which was reckoned to take around three-hundred horsepower from the wheels. Other than the major remodelling of Peterborough and Doncaster, the rest of the journey time improvement was in small doses. I well remember the criticism of several of the works. What is the point, said many commentators, of spending all that money moving the River Great Ouse at Offord just to save a minute? Why realign Maxey curve? Why realign the curve at Newton Hall? Well, we know why now. If these works hadn't been done, there would be no four-hour trains between the Scottish and English capitals today. Our aim is to find similar but smaller projects on the Far North Line that can eat away at journey times and thus make our enhanced service be a true hourly one rather than having to remove station calls to make it work. We need to work out how we can run between Inverness and Dingwall in around twenty-eight minutes and run from Dingwall to Tain and back in fifty-eight. Back in 2008, Ian Coucher told us in Inverness that journey times must be improved on our line. This was repeated by David Simpson, Managing Director Network Rail Scotland, at a talk he gave to the Railway Study Association in London last year. This is our task for 2012.

John Brandon, Convener

YET MORE FORWARD PLANNING REPORTS

Three important reports have been published in the last four months. They are:

- Network Rail's Initial Industry Plan, Scotland (IIPS)
- Transport Scotland's Rail 2014 Public Consultation
- The Scottish Government's Infrastructure Investment Plan 2011 (SGIIP)

Network Rail Scotland has set out its vision of what it could deliver during the next control period (2014-2019) given the funding. This includes its £200M plan to improve journey times and service frequency from Inverness to Aberdeen (InvAb); a £37M upgrade of the Highland Main Line (HML), increasing capacity and reducing journey times; a £50M investment in freight; and a £42M fund to increase level crossing safety, including at the barrier-less AOCLs. This will all be very welcome investment benefiting the Highlands at long last and it is all now in public expectation to be delivered.

Very sadly, the Scottish Government's SGIIP now leaves the timing of their two supposedly "priority" projects up in the air, after we have waited so long! The InvAb scheme which was promised for completion in 2016 is now given an end date of 2030! The HML scheme (announced by the First Minister in Inverness in 2008) is now given an end date of 2025. Government green credentials seem to have been watered down and the emphasis now appears to be on dualling the A9 and the A96. I say, "appears to be" because what is now happening is far from clear. The first big test will be to see if the InvAb scheme gets the expected full funding early in 2012 to allow completion in 2016.

Rail 2014, which asks the public to give their views on the standard of rail services they wish to be specified in the new franchise for ScotRail to commence in 2014, has also provoked controversy. Suggestions that the sleepers might be discontinued and all day trains from England to Scotland go no further north than Edinburgh or Glasgow have generated much comment in the newspapers. Perhaps this was unfair and the consultation document was merely setting out ideas for discussion, perhaps not.

Both Rail 2014 (above) and the IIPS betray a geographical bias in authorship, failing to appreciate the sometimes different perspective in the north and the strategic nature of routes to (and from) all parts of Scotland. The IIPS kindly notes that InvAb would "deliver substantial economic and accessibility benefits beyond the monetised benefits." On Highland Main Line (Phase 2) it considers that the upgrade "will provide better access for the communities of Northern Scotland to employment and business opportunities in central Scotland." That is very true, but completely ignores the benefits to both communities of improved access from the south, which an accelerated 07:00 train arriving in Inverness by 10:00 would particularly foster. Both these routes are strategic to Scotland and the economy of Scotland; they are not just Highland projects.

Scotland as well as the Highlands awaits the connectivity that these long awaited rail projects will bring. FoFNL hopes that the effects will be beneficial north of Inverness too.

Richard Ardern

FNE January 2012

FUTURE PLANS ARE NO PLANS

On 9 September last year, David Stewart, Scottish Labour MSP for the Highlands and Islands, asked whether the Scottish Executive whether had set aside funding for improvements to the rail network on the Far North Line. On 21 September the Minister for Housing and Transport was quite blunt: "There are no rail infrastructure improvements planned at present on the Far North Line." He did, however, offer a virtual carrot by adding that the Scottish Government specification for rail infrastructure works for the period 2014 - 2019 will be set out in the High Level Output Specification in 2012. However, when the Initial Industry Plan for Scotland for that period, setting out what the railway industry feels is necessary for economic growth in, was published on 29 September, there was no mention of lines north of Inverness, although improved rail services between Aberdeen and Inverness and upgrading of the Perth to Inverness line were included.

To a second question from Mr Stewart, asking what plans there were to improve rail times on the Far North Line, Mr Brown could only say that officials from Transport Scotland, Network Rail and ScotRail met regularly to discuss timetable improvements across Scotland, but he did know that plans were being developed for a Wick and Thurso to Inverness train to make an additional station call "to better meet local needs", presumably the 11:31 Alness stop added last December.

FNE September 2012

A QUOTATION WHOSE TIME IS AWAITED

"I hope that in a few years' time we won't be holding ceremonies looking back at 150 years, but hopefully seeing as many people as this at opening ceremonies for new schemes that are being opened on the railway, putting back what was taken away from us in the Sixties."

Ron McAulay, Director (Scotland), Network Rail, speaking at the Nairn 150 celebrations, 9 July 2005.

FRIENDS OF THE FAR NORTH LINE - WHAT WE WISH TO SEE IN CP6

"We must find and exploit real opportunities to reduce journey times"

Iain Coucher, CEO of Network Rail at the FoFNL AGM in Inverness, 30 June 2008

Network Rail (NR) will begin a fresh Route Study (RS) for Scotland shortly after the announcement of the new daytime franchise, expected to be "in the autumn". This paper suggests what it ought to incorporate. It is clear from the experience of how projects are taken forward (or not) that anything absent from NR's RS will not happen. Thus getting projects into the RS, at least as far as being mentioned, is vital. We regard ourselves as a serious contributor to this process and our Recommendations are based on a thoughtful insight and analysis of the present position on the Scottish railway. We return to Iain Coucher's words, taken from his speech over 6 years ago, since when journey times on the FNL have not reduced.

FoFNL will confine its thoughts to matters affecting rural railways in Scotland, and services connecting them to centres of population. It leaves the inter-city railway to others to comment upon.

Transport Scotland (TS) has a public policy commitment to financing the electrification of 100 single-track kilometres (stk) a year once the Edinburgh-Glasgow Improvements Programme (EGIP) is complete, probably by 2019. We expect the routes to be included in this rolling programme to be (in no particular order) Dunblane to Inverness; Perth to Dundee; Edinburgh to Aberdeen; the Fife Circle; the old GSWR route to Carlisle. For operational reasons we expect Aberdeen to Inverness to be electrified also, although we acknowledge that a business case may be hard to make on its own. Our reasoning is that the extended figure-of-eight of the main cities would then be on a single electrified system. We also expect minor electrification infills within the Greater Glasgow area.

If our analysis is correct the only Scottish routes still powered by diesel after about 2030 will be:

- Inverness to Thurso (for Scrabster and Orkney) and Wick (for Gills Bay and Orkney)
- Dingwall to Kyle of Lochalsh (for Skye, Harris and North Uist via Uig)
- Glasgow to Fort William and Mallaig (for Skye, Small Isles, Knoydart and South Uist)
- Crianlarich to Oban (for Mull, Colonsay, Coll, Tiree, South Uist and Barra)
- Glasgow to Stranraer (for Cairnryan, Larne and Belfast)
- Newcraighall to Tweedbank

The last of these will serve a large hinterland with no other access to rail services. Four of the other five all serve important towns which serve as ferry terminals for lifeline island services; the fifth (Stranraer) serves - or could serve - a ferry link to a major city.

We welcome the TS electrification policy, and expect it to start post-EGIP around the start of CP6 and to be concluded early in CP8 at the latest. We accept that diesel-powered trains will serve the six routes above at least until around 2030 and probably well beyond.

Thus it is right to give serious thought now to how services on these lines should be improved in the medium term - ie. in CP6. Improvements should be considered both to infrastructure and to Train Operating Company (TOC) matters - rolling stock and timetables. However it is impossible to separate timetable matters from infrastructure enhancements. There is a hidden danger in asking the question "what does NR need to do to make the current timetable better?". That would tend to cement the current timetable in place for ever: what needs to be asked is the question "what enhancements does NR need to make, perhaps over several years, to deliver the ideal timetable?".

We don't have all the answers, but we can shed some light on how a practical answer may be approached by considering outcomes, and noting existing things which seem to prevent these from happening.

What passengers want most from a rail service is reliability at reasonable cost. Cost is politically-influenced and is outwith the scope of this paper. Passengers wish to board a train when it is advertised and get off when they expect to, either because they have reached their destination or because they have onward travel arrangements. Delivering this reliability is particularly difficult on a single-line railway - there is no need to provide evidence as it is clear that a train which misses its path early in the day can cause disruption, often of increasing severity, throughout the day. The cost to the TOC of compensation, and - worse because it is invisible - to the delayed passengers (because consequential loss is not recoverable) is very large, and in some cases will undoubtedly lead to considerable distress. Preventing such knock-on delays lies at the root of the necessary enhancements.

It is impractical to seek to have the entire length of the six routes doubled, even where the solum still permits this. What is needed is a detailed study on each route of the ideal timetable, and then (and only then) a study of what doubling, and associated signalling, would be needed to deliver it. (FoFNL believes it can suggest the answers on the Far North Line, but we are not experts, and may well overlook important engineering factors: hence the need for this work to be carried out by NR. We are aware that such studies have been carried out in the past - most importantly the Room for Growth study by Scott Wilson of 24 March 2006, now on the TS website; these should be used as a foundation for more thorough work now.) Once this is done and rough costs known it will be possible for funders and passenger groups to argue their case to Government. Very large sums are being committed in Central Scotland to rail enhancements (and vastly larger sums south of the Border); rural and island communities have been left behind in many cases. Caledonian MacBrayne has acquired new vessels, but once the vessel has docked the on-land public transport connection is, in some cases, much as it was 30 years ago - except that it is often much slower, and more expensive.

We acknowledge that more trains run on the six routes than was the case 30 - or even 10 - years ago, but the journeys themselves are less comfortable. We do not expect to see a return to locomotive haulage of Mark 3 stock but nor do we expect to see the present ex-BR Class 15X units in service up to 2030 and beyond unless considerable internal and engineering improvements are carried out. EGIP will release a large fleet of Class 170 units and a sensible refurbishment of these for use on scenic rural routes may be possible. (The new franchise requires the provision of a "tourist train" for some - but curiously not all - of the six routes. It is hoped that details of what this means, and how it will be provided, will accompany the new franchise announcement.) TS in collaboration with Highland Rail Partnership carried out an excellent refurbishment of the Inverness Class 158 fleet some years ago, with input specifically aimed at better provision for tourists, as well as for local long-distance passengers. This model should be adopted for the six routes in the new franchise.

RECOMMENDATIONS:

- **A detailed study, with input from relevant bodies, should be carried out by Network Rail on each of the six routes of the ideal timetable, and then (and only then) a study of what doubling, and associated signalling, would be needed to deliver it.**

- **Immediately the rolling stock details ("tourist train" and others which may also be announced) are known a long-term cascading plan should be drawn up. It is understood that the Department for Transport is set against such thinking in England - all the more reason why Transport Scotland and the new franchisee should show DfT the way.**

- **FoFNL will produce a separate paper outlining its views of the infrastructure enhancements needed on the FNL and Kyle Lines as an input to the process described in Recommendation 1. It is expected that this will follow within 2 months of the franchise announcement.**

This Stations Survey is an excellent example of the kind of work that FoFNL can do. As we are not part of rail provision we can 'step back' and view what's provided from the passengers' point of view. The survey contains too much information to reproduce here but we would urge the reader to go online and find www.fofnl.org.uk/newsletters/16Jan/16jan12.php to see the long list of items covered. The web copy shows in green the items that ScotRail was already working on or agreed straight away to remedy.

FNE January 2016

Stations Survey 2015

FoFNL carried out a survey of all stations on the FNL during August. The report below was sent to ScotRail in October. A reply was received from Phil Verster, MD of ScotRail Alliance setting out what was planned.

In addition to these ScotRail will also install lower counters at ticket offices in Wick and Thurso, and improve cycle parking at Inverness. They will be "looking at" the demolition of the derelict station buildings at Georgemas Junction and Invershin, and "reviewing" the issues surrounding stepping distances. Short of unjustifiably expensive rebuilding of many platforms there are only two simple ways of ameliorating large stepping distances. The method already in use at many platforms - of providing moveable steps - seems the simplest. Building a "Harrington hump" (a raised section of platform) seems unnecessarily costly given the small numbers of passengers boarding or alighting at the affected platforms. We expect the provision of more sets of steps to be the outcome of the review.

FoFNL is pleased to see that the more safety-related matters identified are being attended to, but is disappointed that the installation of tactile edging to modern standards (as at Dingwall) is not being progressed.

The first two categories covered are Network Rail and ScotRail. The third category is 'others':

These are almost entirely concerned with signage between the town centre and the station (in both directions). All stations now display maps of the locality, including the town or village centre, but not everyone can read maps. A finger post outside the station pointing along the road towards the town or village centre would be useful. In many towns, not least Thurso, there is no indication of any kind that there is a railway station - no road sign, no pedestrian fingerpost - until the double arrow (itself of the small kind) is seen. In Wick the station is hidden away and there is only one road sign in the town centre (from the north) bearing a direction to the station. In many smaller villages there is little indication: sometimes a fingerpost with small double arrow at the turning itself, which is often too late to make a safe turning. The Highland Council should examine all these, perhaps by driving from Inverness to Wick and back and observing the lack of signage - a merry day's work on a nice day.

Whoever is responsible for the publication and display of bus timetables should review their practice as it is often poor, inaccurate or non-existent. Presumably someone is paying for this to be done, and if so they should monitor what is being provided (or not provided).

It is not clear who is responsible for the state of the car park at Golspie. In 2008 this was recorded as being well-maintained and well-surfaced. The spate of new buildings, commercial and domestic, since then has rendered the parking area inadequate and poorly maintained. The surface is full of puddles. We have not sought to set out all the many minor irritations there are to users of Inverness station. There is every likelihood that most of these, certainly the structural ones, will be addressed in the chosen redevelopment plan. FoFNL hopes to be able to input ideas when the final plan is chosen, but before it is set in stone. Other nuisances are generally the result of thoughtless behaviour - bad parking, for example - by others, often non-users of the station. Good station planners will seek to design these out where possible.

SOMETIMES BAD THINGS HAPPEN

[Below] Bridge strike, Inverness, February 2008. There is no excuse.
Photo: *Press & Journal*

[Above] Flood damage at Watten, 2006.

[Below right] Bridge strike, Inverness Harbour, 2003.
Photo. Sandy McCook, *Press & Journal*

[Below left] "Please remove that immediately!" Incident at Portgower in March 2013.
Photo: Network Rail

FoFNL Conference 20 years on...

FNE September 2015

Newsletter No.40 Revisited

What happens now...?

Any member who still has a copy of *Newsletter 40* (March 2007) might have a few moments of fun re-reading it. It was a slim extra copy produced in the run-up to the Holyrood elections in May of that year. It started by listing the ten things in an even earlier Newsletter (25, in the run-up to the 2001 General Election, when railway matters in Scotland were still very much a Westminster responsibility) which had set out as *Questions To Ask Your Candidate*. The 2005 article reckoned that one out of the ten (Invernet) had been achieved which, while a good start, was hardly thrilling stuff. The article set out, in a leisurely way, what *The Real Rail Way Ahead: 2007 - 2035*[1] should look like.

And in many ways it was gratifyingly accurate. The 12 things (there had been some inflation) listed were:

1. Do some work on redoubling and/or loops on the FNL and Kyle Line (**no**, but NR might be beginning to think about a loop at Lentran)

2. RETB replacement and colour light signalling as far as Dingwall (**no**, but TS might be thinking about extending the planned HML installation of ERTMS beyond Inverness)

3. Controlled-emission toilets on 158s (**YES**)

4. Further extension of Invernet (**YES**)

5. Inverness-Aberdeen redoubling and/or loops (**no**, but some work is planned in CP5)

6. HML doubling (**no**, but this is clearly in NR planning)

7. Gauge clearance to allow 170s and 22Xs to run on inter-city routes (**no**, but an even better option of having HSTs on these routes by 2019, so scored as a **YES** since better rolling stock was the desired outcome)

8. Replacement rolling stock (partial, but the matter is very much on the table. The new electric sets for EGIP will certainly score a **YES** and the HSTs on the inter-city score a **YES**. Whether the much-vaunted "tourist train" - sexed up 158s - will strike FNL users as anything new is a matter still in the jury room)

9. E-G electrification (**YES**)

10. Waverley Phase II (**YES**, and very fine it is)

11. GSWR doubling (**no**)

12. Initial work on identifying a route for High Speed between Edinburgh and Glasgow (partial, as the idea of HSx is firmly in Scottish Ministers' minds, linking with HS2 and even perhaps (stripping out the pre-election guff) starting to build south from the Central Belt towards some English destination - Newcastle?)

That's 5½ **YES**, and 5 **no**. A lot better than 1 out of 10 last time. Pushing for items 1 and 2 are FoFNL's highest priority now as although there have been several successful predictions their benefits have not been felt up here. Caithness and Sutherland passengers, taxpayers and - occasionally - voters require the pendulum to swing their way. The Central Belt is swallowing up investment (albeit at nothing like the London rate); the Borders are now having their cake. Rail spending per head of population in London exceeds the spending per head in the north of England by a factor of several dozen; it probably exceeds the amount spent per head of population in the north of Scotland by a factor of several hundred. But in 2016 there's another Holyrood election, and this autumn there's the start of the CP6 planning process, so come on, chaps, time for delivery.

Mike Lunan

[1] You can find this on our website: www.fofnl.org.uk/newsletters/0307/030703.php

Verster Visit

Frank Roach, with his HITRANS hat on, invited Phil Verster, Managing Director of the Abellio ScotRail/Network Rail Alliance, to the Far North. He met some of the Committee in Inverness on the

evening of 27 July and travelled north on the 10:38 the following day. By great good fortune this train was a mere 8 minutes late when I joined it at Altnabreac, having used the 13:06 from Thurso to get there. What a boon is the Network Rail "Live Departures" website, for without it and its disclosure that the 10:38 was indeed running that day I might have had to spend another 4 hours there. Delightful though it be, its attractions pall quite quickly, especially in midge weather.

Phil and I discussed various things in the 25 minutes before we arrived at Thurso. I reminded him that some of the actions he agreed following last year's Station Survey were still incomplete, and he welcomed the reminder. These are principally the painting of safety white lines at most of the stations, and the installation of tactile edging at Tain. This is needed because of the opening of Platform 1864 - location of the AGM this year (and very fine it is, too - eat there when you are next in the area) - and the added risk of those who have dined too well being unaware of the drop onto the line. I also pressed on him our view of the Scotland Route Study and the great importance we attach to the Lentran Loop. He agreed that there needed to be some doubling

Phil Verster, Mike Lunan and Frank Roach with train conductor, Ewan Anderson

between Inverness and Muir of Ord (as the Study sets out), but that the decision lay with the politicians.

On arrival at Thurso I was able to point out the paucity of convenient parking and - a continuing irritation to one member - the odd EXIT signage which directs the unwary to a locked door 50 yards away. The arrow pointing up was photographed, and it is to be hoped that it is replaced by one pointing left. We are promised a Customer Information Screen at Thurso (and at Wick), so these might be enjoyed soon.

It's clear that Abellio are well aware of the needs of the FNL, articulated here and elsewhere by FoFNL, and the warmth with which we exchanged thoughts bodes well for seeing improvements when funds become available. The Alliance's job is doing the work when it's programmed: ours is making sure that it gets programmed in the 2019-24 Control Period.

Mike Lunan

Forsinard Sation - "wet bed", July 2016. Phil Verster acknowledged that this was listed in the 2015 Station Survey and needs to be fixed.

GLAZEBROOK REPORT

A major event for us in the autumn was the publication on 16 October of a report by rail consultant Tony Glazebrook.

Tony explained that his *modus operandi* would be to ride the whole route in the cab and to have discussions with as many of the people doing the job of running the Far North Line and others directly involved in various capacities as possible. Permission had to be sought from the ScotRail/Network Rail Alliance and was readily given, along with full co-operation.

Tony concluded his report as follows:

"An intensely positive attitude, unparalleled commitment and boundless patience were very evident qualities in everyone that I was fortunate to meet. The FNL exists because of them."

Tony's report, which I urge you to read, is available at www.fofnl.org.uk/archives/Aliona-FoFNL-study-16.10.16.pdf.

The report covers every aspect of the operation of the FNL in great detail, listing problems and suggesting remedies. It provides FoFNL and the politicians who oversee the provision of rail transport, with the information needed to work for improvements. Phil Verster, Managing Director, ScotRail Alliance, responded immediately to the report and asked his teams to action specific issues that arose.

In the report's summary Tony Glazebrook lists the problems and recommends solutions. Among many other issues, he identifies a key cause of the chronic paralysis that affects the FNL in addressing problems:

Management: There is no clarity on who has the authority to make things actually happen. Indeed, despite the frequent discussions on everything that already is known to cause the never-ending FNL problems, there is very little to show for it. If anything, performance is declining still further. There is a lot of good work and analysis ongoing but no apparent focus to bring the system under control, let alone to improve it. This needs urgent attention.

Recommendation: *For clarity to be brought to the identity of the action leader at least at local level and for that role to be afforded the necessary authority.*

ScotRail has already made a start on this by giving Derek Glasgow overall responsibility for the running of the Far North Line.

Among other memorable quotes are these:

Timetable: It is disadvantageous to FNL economics that end-to-end journey times in the current timetable are some 30 minutes longer than in around 2000! The train from Inverness to Thurso takes between 3¾ and 4 hours, and to Wick between 4¼ and 4½ hours. Even with 11 stops, the X99 bus service takes only 3 hours from Inverness to Thurso or Wick, whilst driving the same route takes only 2½ hours to Thurso or 2¼ to Wick.

Recommendation: *For a single individual to be charged with the task of leading the drive for route improvements that aims, at the very least, within the next 5 years to restore end-to-end FNL journey times to their level in the year 2000.*

Infrastructure Costs: The reason for the apparently high costs for railway infrastructure changes and investment is worthy of examination and justification, especially in areas where the 'fare box' revenue cannot cover those costs. It is unclear how the costs are built up and only a critical examination of such would enable a reasonable balance to be achieved between cost and available resource.

Recommendation: *For NR to choose a sample project from each of the Signalling and Track disciplines and provide a breakdown showing how the apparently high costs are derived.*

Ian Budd

STEAM VISITORS

The Great Britain IV

Stanier 'Black 5s' 44871 and 45407 running round the train at Georgemas Junction on 18 April 2011.

Photo: Mike Lunan

Thomson B1, 61306, *Mayflower*, leading the *Highlands & Islands Explorer* tour out of Dunrobin Castle Station on 11 May 2019.

Photo: Daniel Brittain-Catlin

The Great Britain IV

Ready to leave Georgemas Junction on 18 April 2011.

Photo: Mike Lunan

Four Meetings and a RESULT!

Fergus Ewing announces *Review Team* for FNL - ScotRail, Network Rail, HITRANS and FoFNL

Report of four meetings attended on 15 and 16 December 2016

1   **With Humza Yousaf MSP, Minister of Transport.** (Also there, Bob Barnes-Watts of FoFNL and Rose Tweedale of Transport Scotland [TS].) We gave the Minister a copy of a document entitled The Lentran Loop (see below) which he welcomed. He agreed to write officially to The Highland Council and to HITRANS pressing them to look seriously at the case, including a STAG appraisal - this was "the best way forward". He accepted that making a business case is beyond the competence of FoFNL. He assured us that he had "a sympathetic ear", and was pleased that FoFNL had cross-party support from MSPs.

2   **With Bill Reeve, Director of Rail at TS.** He explained a great deal of what was going on in the e-ticketing area. He told us that FoFNL "punched above [our] weight" and acknowledged the strength of our cross-party support among our VPs. My idea of bolting on an order for new DMUs to the order placed by Northern Rail would apparently be illegal, so I shall stop banging that particular drum. However he was "not against" more new DMUs "in due course". This is a big step forward from the prevailing view in the industry that no-one would manufacture new diesel kit at an affordable price. (We should not read any degree of "soon" into this, however - the 158s will be our stock on the FNL for a decade or more.) He asked us about freight possibilities, but apart from the timber traffic it is hard to see where any southbound load will emerge. He noted that, whereas summer passenger numbers rose significantly on the Kyle line and the Oban/For William/Mallaig services, this did not happen on the FNL. Why not? I suggested tapping into the Scrabster cruise ships with a nice steam train to Wick and back, with a bus to John o'Groats. (I will talk to Scrabster to see whether this might fly, or whether it is just pie in the sky.)

3   **Frank Roach's second Points North conference.** This had a truly excellent line-up of speakers - chosen by Frank to explain specific aspects of FNL performance. First was Alex Sharkey, the top NR man in our area. He gave a very instructive presentation about what NR plans to do in the balance of CP5 (up to March 2019) - most of which will be wholly invisible to passengers of course. All the more reason for our knowing about it. Derek Glasgow referred to Tony Glazebrook's consultancy report and spoke about the 158 refurbishment programme, which will be complete in July 2017. Once the EGIP EMUs are up and running the plan is that the Inverness fleet of 158s will never travel south of Inverness (except towards Aberdeen/Montrose). Ian Whiteley went into detail about the RETB improvements (which seem to me, on the basis of two journeys, to allow late-running to be recovered more quickly: 9 minutes late at Tain becoming on-time at Inverness). Phil Verster said that HLOS will focus on outcomes, and reduced end-to-end timings on the FNL ought to be part of this. There was a team working on speeds within loops. Simon Constable (the safety and LX king) told us of increased line-speeds at 4 LXs, but said that speed might have to be reduced at 2 others because of increased road traffic. He outlined planned changes at Delny and in Dingwall. This was the most useful two hours I have spent at a railway conference in the 17-odd years I have been attending them.

4   **The Rail Stakeholder Conference.** Cabinet Secretary Fergus Ewing MSP was the main speaker. He announced that he was setting up a "Review Team" (not, he said, a Task Force) to consider the FNL. It would have immediate and longer term outputs. In the short term how to improve performance, in the longer term seeking major changes and improvements. He noted that NR's Route Strategy had some double tracking between Inverness and Dingwall suggested for CP6 or CP7 and said that "capital investment, more medium and long term, should be in CP6". He announced that the Review Team would comprise ScotRail, NR, HITRANS - and FoFNL. Frazer Henderson (Head of Rail Policy at TS) outlined the TS Consultation on the HLOS process. Several points were clarified. We then heard about progress on the Aberdeen-Inverness and HML enhancements. We were told that the May 2017 timetable for the

FNL/Kyle lines would "stabilize" and set performance "to acceptable levels". Difficult word acceptable: it certainly won't see a return to 2000 timings, some 30 minutes faster than they are now. This is a murky area, and exploring it for solutions will doubtless be a major part of the "immediate" task of the Review Team. One of the twinkles in Frank's eyes - a depot at Elgin - seems to be on stream for December 2018. The first ex-GWR HST will arrive for driver training in 2017, and the first refurbished set will be delivered in "spring 2018". On being pressed about delays in releasing the sets following the electrification fiasco on the GWR the reply was "we have a contract". It will be interesting to see whether the contract is delivered according to the letter, or if DfT and TS come to an agreement. If there is to be a delay there must be compensation - £1 million a day seems sufficiently punishing to focus minds. Peter Strachan showed us pictures, taken only the day before, of his new Sleeper trains being built in Spain. The interior fitment is not just a step up from the existing kit (itself nicer, and better cared-for, than it used to be), but a whole flight of stairs better. It will be interesting to see the use made of the double bed. (Perhaps I might rephrase that.) To round off the day we saw plans for the upgrade of Inverness Station.

Mike Lunan

FNE January 2017

FoFNL Submission for 2017 HLOS

The Lentran Loop

Until it was singled by BR 50 years ago that part of the FNL immediately to the north of the Clachnaharry Swing Bridge was double track for six miles. The solum is still extant. FoFNL is calling for some degree of infrastructure enhancement in this location. The bridge carrying the A862 over the railway some 4 miles from the Swing Bridge prevents double track there. The settlement at Lentran is roughly half-way between Inverness and Muir of Ord, now the first place north of Inverness where trains may pass (13 miles, usually taking 21 minutes to traverse). Were trains able to pass in this neighbourhood late-running southbound trains would have a significantly reduced impact on the delivery of the timetable for the rest of the day.

The most damaging, and sadly not infrequent, occurrence is when the first train from Caithness (having left Wick at 06:18) reaches Muir of Ord more than around 15 minutes after its scheduled time of 10:14. In order to make maximum use of the single track between there and Inverness the 10:38 departure to Wick and the 11:00 departure to Kyle of Lochalsh are flighted, with the Kyle train not leaving Muir of Ord until 11:21. Thus by the time the delayed Wick train is allowed to proceed - perhaps not until 11:22 at the earliest - it will not arrive at Inverness until 11:43, some 69 minutes late. Connections to Aberdeen and the Central Belt have been missed, as have many appointments, not least at Raigmore Hospital. While a passing place - or better still a dynamic loop 2 or 3 miles long - would not eliminate this, it would allow the Wick train to reach Inverness before the Kyle departure, and thus arrive only 25 or so minutes late. The knock-on effect of a late arrival naturally makes the use of the late set for other services harder to achieve, and a late departure with that set will mean that all services are likely not to present at passing places at the correct time for the rest of the day.

In the Scotland Route Study Network Rail (NR) states (p53) "The rail network north of Inverness ... provides "lifeline" services to rural communities, consequently connectivity and resilience are key" (emphasis added). Later (p83) one of the Far North Enhancements is "Inverness to Dingwall additional loop to provide greater flexibility to pass trains". A long-term objective (p147) is for "1 opportunity to travel every other hour [between Inverness and Wick]". If the "day" is taken to mean roughly what it does now (with trains running on the FNL between 06:18 and 22:52 - say 16 hours) that will mean at least 6 services each way each weekday: far beyond the current capability of the route). However, the study does give itself until 2043 to deliver this "output".

When we reach the meat of the study (p194) there is no sign of any plan to provide a loop south of

Dingwall. 6.6.21 suggests a possible (green) plan to install double track between Dingwall and Invergordon in CP6. While FoFNL would applaud this, we do not believe it will do anything to address the problem of the 21-minute single section through Lentran. 6.6.19 suggests re-signalling between Inverness and Dingwall, but not until CP7 - we suggest a shorter time-scale.

The consultation paper "The Far North Line: a performance study", commissioned from Aliona Ltd in October 2016, recommends (p15) that NR's proposed re-signalling between Inverness and Dingwall could allow a passing loop to be signalled using what it describes as the "Aviemore solution". Scottish Ministers and Transport Scotland have copies of this paper. On p23 it goes on to suggest that comparative costings are obtained for providing a Lentran loop as part of any re-signalling, or as a stand-alone scheme retaining RETB. FoFNL supports this approach as likely to constrain costs.

At FoFNL's Annual Conference in Inverness in June 2008 Iain Coucher, then CEO of NR, said, in the context of the FNL "We must find and exploit real opportunities to reduce journey times". While the Lentran Loop will not of itself reduce journey times, it will permit more robust delivery of the timetable. NR has, in the study, "found" opportunities: it must now be instructed to "exploit" them.

We urge Transport Scotland and Scottish Ministers to include the Lentran Loop in its HLOS in June 2017.

Mike Lunan's second 'swansong'!

FNE January 2018

HEADCODE

2018 will be a memorable year for Scotland's railway. Many projects with a long lead-time will come to fruition. Already electric trains are running between Queen Street and Waverley, and the new trains ordered are being delivered. Work to electrify the route through Shotts is now well under way. The HSTs rescued from GWR will start to appear on other Inter-City routes this year, affording a substantial increase in comfort and convenience for passengers. ASR has had to put up with a lot of flak, some of it undeserved, but with any luck 2018 will be the year which brings compliments and passenger appreciation.

The new Sleeper coaches will arrive too, and ought to be delivering the full timetable by the end of the year. Here the improvement in accommodation will be astonishing, and there will be many of us keenly anticipating our first overnight journey. The plan to introduce a sleeper service from Thurso ("for Orkney") to Edinburgh using the best of the displaced rolling stock should move closer to fulfilment - fingers crossed. VTEC will be introducing their Azuma fleet this year. A unit has been as far north as Inverness already. The electric version operating south from Edinburgh will shave a useful amount of time from the current timetable; we awaited, with interest, detailed timings for the much more challenging bi-mode performance over the hilly HML. A table showing a crucial part of the 15 January run appears on page 10. The technical press has been pessimistic about the suggested uprating of the diesel motors' output for reasons not unconnected with the technical press's unhappiness that the trains were ordered by the DfT (who, you will not have failed to notice, neither operate trains nor have 'customers'). And here? The Review Team met, as reported here, in May 2017 and NR were to go and put flesh on their outline proposals for an improved timetable, and generally to give us a better railway. The putting-on of flesh is going to take as long as it would in real life: the next meeting will be in February, too late for its outcome to be reported here. But a process which occupies the finest minds in NR (Scotland) for nine months surely cannot produce a mere mouse.

So let me say, for what I'm confident will be the last time -

THE LENTRAN LOOP MUST BE BUILT

As Bugs Bunny was fond of saying "That's all, folks!"

Mike Lunan

> The final extract in *FoFNL 25* - the most recent *Headcode* - shows that, as Bob Barnes-Watts said in 2018, "FoFNL realises that the line does not exist in splendid isolation, hence the enormous effort expended over the past 24 years in reminding those in control of both the purse and policy strings of their responsibility to continue the improvements to the routes feeding the North Highland Lines as a whole."

FNE September 2019

Headcode

The Parliamentary Questions section of *Far North Express* is normally given without comment - not least in order to maintain our politically neutral status as campaigners. I'm going to make an exception on this occasion because the two recent exchanges in the Scottish Parliament illustrate the problems of both rail campaigners and party politicians.

In the background is a reluctance to hint at giving any ground in relation to reducing the roads programme. The Deputy First Minister said that recent work to improve the Highland Main Line is part of a "balanced package". In fact, the HML is getting slower. In the new timetable, the longest journey time from Inverness to Edinburgh has increased to 3 hours 46 minutes . This is a whole hour longer than the 2 hours 45 minutes promised by Alex Salmond in 2008 for the fastest services. He also stated that by 2012 the average journey time would be only 3 hours. Under current Government Policy, achieving this promise will have been delayed by 13 years to 2025.

On the subject of freight The Cabinet Secretary for Transport, Infrastructure and Connectivity said on 12 June, "We will continue to do everything that we can to encourage commercial businesses to make use of the rail freight options that are available to them." This ignores the fact that until there is better infrastructure to allow more freight paths and longer trains, the options available are very limited. This applies to all the single track railways in Scotland. It is revealing that he also felt it necessary to say that he did "not know whether it is now official Labour Party policy to cut the roads budget and transfer that money to rail instead" and "I suspect that, in later questions, members will also ask me to make more investment in roads."

As mentioned elsewhere in this edition, we were delighted to hear the First Minister, on 5 September, rise to the challenge to "be bold in the Climate Emergency and take funds out of new, big, roads projects and invest them in public transport instead".

The reason we never stop talking about the single-track HML is that many of our northbound services are directly affected by holding departures from Inverness, particularly the 18:31, to wait for late-running trains from the south. If the HML was mostly double-track this would cease to be a problem. We have to get the message across:

Main lines linking important cities in Scotland must not remain single track.

Ian Budd

The Highland Main Line at Pitlochry Station on 26 March 2019 after work on the passing loop was completed.

This is how Scottish inter-city lines must be from end-to-end, not just at passing-places.

Photo: Network Rail

FoFNL Policy Aims for Future Rail Services

The policy aims which follow are all achievable within a reasonably short time scale, but come at a cost. This may be a capital or a running cost, or both. How acceptable such costs will be to Government and to taxpayers will depend on various factors, not least the ability of the Government and the railway industry to keep costs under control and to show that railway services do give value for money.

However, on the Highland lines, some costs have, in the past, been reduced to such a level that the dependability of services, and hence passenger confidence, have been compromised. That is not the way to run the railway or indeed any service to the public.

It is important not to look at railway services too narrowly in terms of their costs and also to consider the benefits railway services provide to the local economy in both economic and social terms. The 2004 Steer Davies Gleave (now known as "Steer") report on the value of rail to the Highlands, elucidated some of these issues and has perhaps even greater relevance today.

The policy document below is not an uncosted immediate wish list. It merely states our position on many of the improvements which could be made to the Far North Line and connecting train services through Inverness if there is the will to do so.

We are delighted with the success of the Far North Line Review Team, established in 2016 by Fergus Ewing, Cabinet Secretary for the Rural Economy. This was in response to the report on all aspects of the line carried out that year by Tony Glazebrook. We hope that the Scottish Government will soon have control over a devolved Network Rail Scotland.

We would urge the Scottish Government now to prioritise the removal of the many capacity constraints on the single track lines serving Inverness from the rest of the Scottish network and equally to seek the design of more suitable trains which, in the light of the declaration in 2019 of a "Climate Emergency", will need to be electrically powered in some form, perhaps using hydrogen. The market for such trains would extend far wider, e.g. West Highland Line, Settle & Carlisle, Cambrian Coast and lines in Devon & Cornwall.

Passenger travel by rail is finding an increasing market and rail must also provide a greater proportion of freight movement. Railways will have a bright future particularly if the right investment decisions are made and all players focus on providing the passenger with an enjoyable travel environment and experience.

Policies

Passengers

We would like to see that the railway service providers (Transport Scotland, Network Rail and the franchise holder) achieve the following in respect of passengers:

1. Services

    1.1 Implement the rail/ferry connections through Thurso to and from Orkney to reflect the increased pattern of ferry services.

    1.2 Secure the introduction, in conjunction with 1.1 above, of a dedicated connecting bus service between Thurso station and Scrabster harbour.

    1.3 Secure the introduction of connecting bus services from the seaboard villages to Fearn station, likewise the Dornoch to Tain bus service to reflect the increased rail service frequency under Invernet.

    1.4 Enhance services south of Inverness by the introduction of sub 3-hour express services to Edinburgh and Glasgow with an hourly frequency.

    1.5 Enhance the connections eastwards by the introduction of the hourly frequency through Moray to Aberdeen with a no more than 2 hour total journey time.

    1.6 Continue and improve catering services on all Inverness/Wick services.

1.7   Continue to provide and improve connections to, and collaboration with, the Sleeper and the Highland Chieftain services especially when perturbations occur.

2. Rolling Stock

Our clear overall preference would be for a new build of rolling stock suitable for and appropriate to long distance rural scenic routes throughout the UK. The Far North Line therefore requires new trains with the following characteristics, in that they will have:

2.1   Sufficient power, good gearing, and adhesion appropriate for use on steep gradients and tight curves.

2.2   Enough weight to be effective in all adverse weather conditions.

2.3   Appropriate tourist viewing.

2.4   Draught free passenger cabins.

2.5   Sets with a minimum of three carriages, with one toilet in each.

2.6   Comfortable seating approved beforehand by a representative group of the passengers who will be using these trains.

2.7   Storage space for 6 bicycles per train set.

2.8   Sufficient luggage space to accommodate rucksacks and other bulky items of baggage.

3. Stations

3.1   Re-open the station at Evanton.

3.2   Re-open the station at Halkirk in conjunction with the construction of the Georgemas curve.

3.3   Consider staffing Tain for Invernet services.

3.4   Expand the car-parking facilities at Dingwall, Invergordon, Fearn and Tain stations.

3.5   Provide cycle lockers and Sheffield racks at Invernet stations.

3.6   Provide waiting facilities, which are wind and watertight, well lit and where possible, heated.

3.7   Ensure that adequate lavatory facilities are available for passengers using all services.

3.8   Provide telephone contact with a controller in Inverness (not Dunfermline) for use at times of late running.

3.9   Provide disabled access at stations.

3.10   Encourage local residents and other interested parties in supporting the upkeep of local stations.

4. Infrastructure Improvements

4.1   Additional track/loop between Inverness and Dingwall.

4.2   Additional track/loop between Dingwall and Invergordon.

4.3   Additional track/loop between Helmsdale and Forsinard.

4.4   Construct a curve at Georgemas taking trains between Thurso and the south to avoid trains having to reverse.

5. Fares and Marketing

- The fare structure must give due weighting to the average per capita income within the catchment area of the far north line.
- Maintain the Highland Railcard's fifty percent concession for local residents.

- Introduce, in conjunction with Invernet, day return fares from Tain south through to Edinburgh, Glasgow, and Aberdeen.
- Target marketing in advance of the introduction of a new service or facility e.g. Invernet.
- Focus marketing at communities and users along the line, and FoFNL would be willing to assist with this as we have done in the past.
- Agree with Highland Council a system for charging senior citizen rail fares such that there is parity between rail and bus fare charging.

Freight

1. Infrastructure

We would like to see that Transport Scotland and/or Network Rail achieve the following in respect of freight transport infrastructure:

1.1 Removal of severe speed restrictions for loco-hauled trains, which limit freight paths and constrain the overall capacity of the line.

1.2 Improvement of line capacity through new crossing loops and/or dynamic loops.

1.3 Enhancement of line capability in terms of 'loading gauge' (and axle weights north of Invergordon).

1.4 Improvement of line capacity and capability (including loading gauge and axle weights) on the Highland Main Line linking the Far North Line to the Central Belt.

1.5 Protection, in conjunction with The Highland Council, of all relevant land for future rail freight needs.

1.6 Support for the development / re-development of rail freight terminal facilities at strategic locations such as Invergordon Distillery, Lairg and Georgemas Junction.

1.7 Support for innovative rail haulage and handling methods for the movement of timber from low-cost terminals.

2. Services

We would like to see the Scottish Government achieve the following in respect of freight services:

2.1 Recognition of the major contribution which rail freight can make to meeting the challenge of the climate emergency.

2.2 Institute innovative grant funding to help new rail freight services establish commercial viability.

2.3 Provision of support for the continuation and development of existing nuclear and pipes traffic on the FNL, and encourage moves to secure additional traffic such as bulk spirit, domestic waste, liquid natural gas, scrap steel, supermarket supplies, timber, etc

2.4 Provision of support for the development of small freight / parcels service on passenger trains between Inverness and Thurso / Wick.

We would like to see The Highland Council promote rail freight in its Development Plans.

Postscript

We firmly believe in the Far North Line's future as a vital and strategic link between Orkney, Caithness and Sutherland and the rest of Great Britain and Europe and that it deserves continued investment. The Highlands and Islands Enterprise network and the Highland Council have, under the Scottish Government, responsibilities for the social, economic and environmental health of the far north communities and in this the line plays its part.

Policy reaffirmed 14-10-2019.

FAR NORTH LINE
WINDOW GAZER'S GUIDE

The Friends of the Far North Line group was involved with the specification for refurbishing the Inverness allocation of class 158 trains in 2007 which created more bike and luggage space. All the comfortable new Grammer seats were aligned with the windows, an essential for a scenic railway.

Photo: Richard Ardern

Leaving Inverness station, the train is soon on the new Ness Viaduct (which replaces the one swept away in 1989) over the river at the inward end of the harbour. There might be shipping to see or, depending on the state of the tide, the sheer rush of water to marvel at. The Beauly Firth is reached just before the Caledonian Canal swing bridge at Clachnaharry Lock which the train clunks over at 10 mph.

Once the former fishing village of Clachnaharry is passed, the view opens out up to the head of the Firth with Ben Wyvis dominant in the background beyond the Black Isle peninsula. The sea sometimes freezes as far out as the canal sea lock and when the tide is full or the sea pastel blue, this is one of the most inspiring views on the line. Passengers should sit on the right hand (coastal) side of the train. Further along near Lentran is a great place to spot wading birds of all kinds particularly on an incoming tide.

Beauly and Conon Bridge are two of the shortest platforms in Britain and passengers have to use one of the middle doors. The small addition to the Beauly stationmaster's house used to be Lord Lovat's private waiting room. The golf course approaching Muir of Ord was once the great tryst where cattle from the Highlands were gathered together before being driven south to market. Until 1960, the Muir was the junction for a branch line to Fortrose. Ben Wyvis now dominates the view from the left hand side of the train all the way to Dingwall and it is a good area to spot

Photo: Dave Conner

the red kites reintroduced some 20 years ago. Conon Bridge was reopened in 2013 and but for WW1 intervening would have been the junction with a branch for Cromarty.

Dingwall, the county town of Ross-shire, has a new agricultural mart building with tearoom and exhibition on cattle droving. It used to be a busy station with an engine shed and it is the junction for the line to Kyle of Lochalsh which heads off to the left. We now travel along the shores of the Cromarty Firth past the Cromarty causeway which was one of three estuarial crossings which have considerably shortened the A9 road to the north to the detriment of the railway. The Fyrish monument on top of the hill to the left looks like a collection of Lowry's matchstick men and contrasts with the modern windfarm. Alness is another reopened station famous for its floral displays.

Nearing Invergordon, offshore oil platforms may already have been spotted. Offshore maintenance is a big industry in the Cromarty Firth as is passenger traffic from the biggest cruise liners in the world which use Invergordon's deep water pier regularly throughout the summer. Invergordon is a former naval base (with a mutiny in 1931), and used to have an aluminium smelter but now has a wood pellet manufacturer on the industrial site to the left. To the right we can see the entrance to the Cromarty Firth between the two headlands known as the Sutors. Beneath the North Sutor is the former oil fabrication yard at Nigg now used for ship repair. Rich level farmland extends all the way to Tain.

At Tain we start to travel along the Dornoch Firth with views north along the coast of Sutherland which we will not reach for another hour. The 1991 Dornoch Bridge for the A9 was built so that a railway bridge could be erected alongside, a scheme which British Rail promoted. This fell short by a £4m contribution required from the Scottish Office which was not independent or much involved in railways in those days.

Photo: Graeme Smith

Tain is a former Royal Burgh, a pleasant town with an interesting museum and former terminus of the local train service to Inverness which ceased when the line was rationalised in 1960. The station buildings have been superbly restored as a restaurant named Platform 1864. Just to the north is the Glenmorangie distillery which has been extended recently and, further on, another at Edderton. Steel magnate Andrew Carnegie's former home, Skibo Castle, is visible across the water between the trees but you have to be quick to see it. Ardgay used to be named for the town of Bonar Bridge at the head of the estuary on the opposite shore. The railway reached this point in October 1864.

We are now in Sutherland, and the continuation and completion of the line to Wick and Thurso took another 10 years and was achieved largely due to the efforts of the Duke of Sutherland. Passing through the attractive wayside station at Culrain we cross the Oykel Viaduct and go through Invershin, another by-request halt. Dominating the view is Carbisdale Castle on a crag on the left. Until recently this was a youth hostel, but millions of pounds of repairs needed on the roof have brought about its closure. It was built as a

Photo: Span Engineering

Photo: Swan-Scot

flamboyant piece of one-upmanship on the Duke by a Dowager Duchess.

Up the hill towards Lairg, the scenery changes to open moorland and hill grazing. Lairg Station is two miles above the village and was formerly an interchange point for passengers and mails to places like Tongue and Lochinver on the north and west coasts. The bus connection is now more limited. The line turns south east, over the summit and down the glen through Rogart to Strath Fleet meeting up with the A9 again at The Mound, once a junction for the 1902 light railway to Dornoch which closed in 1960. Loch Fleet is a National Nature Reserve and another good place to watch for bird life, seals and maybe an otter.

Photo: Daniel Brittain-Catlin

Entering Golspie, the line hugs the coast and the train may then stop at the request halt at Dunrobin Castle. This was the seat of the Duke and is open to the public from April to October. The Victorian museum in the gardens is a fascinating period piece and the wooden station building is most attractive and sometimes open as a railway museum. The next stop is Brora where there used to be a woollen mill and earlier a brick works and coal mine which didn't close until the 1970s. This hive of industry created the earliest (wooden) railway in the north in the 1770s between the mine and the harbour.

The next 15 minutes is one of the highlights of the journey as the line runs along the coastline of sandy beaches giving way eventually to rocky shores. Seals are plentiful, as are rabbits. The extensive views stretch more than 25 miles out to sea past Tarbat Ness lighthouse to the Moray Coast. To the north when nearing Helmsdale the huge 84 turbine offshore wind farm may be seen. It has replaced the three installations of the former Beatrice Oil Field.

Photo: Dunrobin Castle Collection

The fishing village of Helmsdale has the extensive Timespan Museum which includes material on the 1869 Sutherland Goldrush. The station building is now a self catering unit sleeping up to ten people. The line turns inland along the Strath of Kildonan and is at its most beautiful during May when the yellow gorse and broom are in full flower. The Helmsdale River is renowned for its salmon fishing and red deer are evident most of the year. Kildonan is the nearest station to the gold panning sites. It is a long way to the next passing place, not at Kinbrace, but at Forsinard. Here there is an RSPB reserve with a visitor centre and viewing tower with walks to experience the peaty Flow Country with sphagnum moss, sundew flowers and rare birds such as the Greenshank. World Heritage status is being sought for this area.

On over the moors past County March Summit we cross in to Caithness and through the remote station of Altnabreac. Looking south we can see the monadnocks of Morven and Ben Alisky sticking up above the peaty and rocky landscape.